GARDEN COLOUR SERIES

THE GARDEN HANDYMAN

Richard Wiles

AURA
EDITIONS

Endpapers *A brick-built planter is the ideal way to incorporate raised flower beds in your garden. It's neat, tidy and easier to tend than a simple mound.*

Title-page *A well-ordered garden shed is the best place to store your tools and equipment where they'll be safe and dry. Choose size sensibly and you'll have a handy potting shed, too.*

Right *Just some of the basic ingredients of garden construction: sand, cement and aggregates. From these materials your garden can take on its definite shape and structure.*

Series Editor: Susan Conder
Editor: Eluned James
Art Editor: Caroline Dewing

Published by
Aura Editions
2 Derby Road
Greenford, Middlesex

ISBN 0 86307 275 5

Typeset in Ehrhardt 453 by Walkergate Press, Anlaby
Printed and bound in Hong Kong by Dai Nippon
Printing Company

CONTENTS

INTRODUCTION

Creating a successful, well-kempt garden relies on thorough groundwork and constant attention to the daily needs of the plot. Be properly organised and enjoy its special pleasures.

Running a garden involves so much more than coaxing out beautiful blooms, grooming a lush lawn, or keeping a hedge in trim. Before you can even begin to plant out the plot or to sow your first seeds, you have to decide exactly what type of garden you want, what it will contain and how it will look.

The garden consists of many features which are reliant on each other: if one should fall by the wayside, the rest tend to follow. So it's very important to spend a lot of time on creating and maintaining an orderly plot.

Starting with the down-to-earth basics, you will need to know how to style your plot to suit your preferences – whether you want a formal courtyard-style garden with a large, paved area or a more informal effect with different-shaped flower beds and wild shrubberies and undergrowth. You may decide on a functional, neat and orderly site with a well-defined lawn, vegetable patch and planting beds or alternatively a garden that is full of colour and scent that is a joy for everybody to behold.

Identifying soil types or spotting the cause of a poorly-drained site, are some of the early gardening techniques that are easy to learn and put into practice.

Many different and versatile building materials are available for use in the garden. They can help to define the various areas of the garden: you will discover that there is so much you can do using bricks, concrete or timber, without being an expert bricklayer, builder or carpenter. Laying crazy paving or perhaps building a brick wall are tasks that can be easily undertaken and which can really enhance your garden.

Providing the garden with electric lighting, for the shed, patio and garden tools or water for nourishing your crops and blooms, should not be beyond the capabilities of the average, practical gardener. Gardening activities can then be extended beyond the daylight hours – your potting shed can become a warm, light place to work. No longer will you have to traipse through the house with watering cans or use the kitchen tap for a hosepipe – your garden can have its own tap and benefit from its own personal supply of water.

Apart from the regular weeding, pruning, mowing and watering that are very necessary for the upkeep of the garden, there will always be problems with pests, diseases and inclement weather. Pests and diseases, however, can be controlled, and often averted, by keeping a careful watch on all the plants and shrubs in the garden. Persistent pests can be kept at bay with the use of insecticides and repellents, which are easily available from garden centres and DIY shops. Plant disease is difficult to cure and once established all affected plants should be destroyed as soon as possible to protect the rest of the garden.

Once your garden is formed and maturing, and you are involved with the daily task of keeping it running smoothly, you will find that constant maintenance is of utmost importance: you should survey the site regularly to look for any danger signals. Inspect the boundaries for wind damage, for example, and beware of the onset of rot and general dilapidation caused by the passing of time and adverse weather conditions. Repairs throughout the garden should not prove to be difficult, you will soon find your self capable of fitting a new pane of glass in the greenhouse, replacing a rotten fence post, or maybe re-laying a subsided path or driveway.

Well-maintained tools and equipment should be one of the gardener's prime considerations. They should always be cleaned thoroughly after use and, where necessary, regularly sharpened and oiled. If they are neglected your garden will suffer.

When it comes to tackling more complex garden projects, you can hire equipment and machinery so that you can complete the job more quickly. A concrete mixer, for example, can be a great help when you have a large area of concrete to complete.

Choosing garden furniture can be an enjoyable pastime. You can spend some time looking at the many different styles that are available and decide what you want to buy or possibly make yourself. Basic rustic, wooden furniture has a country charm and can be easy to make. Modern, tubular furniture, alternatively, is easy to clean and comes in a variety of fabrics.

When your garden is running like clockwork, you can leave your regular chores for a while and spend some time just relaxing and enjoying your well-run garden.

Opposite *Many small building projects, using many different materials, can be undertaken in your garden to improve and enhance its features.*

CHAPTER 1

DOWN-TO-EARTH BASICS

Whether you want to remodel your garden, improve poor drainage or simply bolster the soil's natural structure and resources, you'll find that basic, sound groundwork reaps the best results.

Opposite *Don't settle for a garden that's the wrong shape: careful cutting-and-filling can alter its profile to suit your requirements.*

Below *Drive a timber peg into the ground to the level you want using a club hammer.*

Bottom *Check that the pegs are at the same depth by spanning their tops with a long straightedge plank and spirit level, then carefully adjust the soil level to the peg heights.*

The secret of a successful garden lies in thorough preparation of the site. Without the initial groundwork your plot will be plagued by ailments and problems.

A steeply sloping garden, for instance, means poor access – especially with equipment such as a lawnmower or wheelbarrow; an entirely flat garden, however, may actually benefit from the introduction of changes of level. Remodelling the earth to improve unsatisfactory conditions is quite straightforward, if laborious.

Even if you don't need to alter the contours of the ground, it may be necessary to improve inadequate drainage to promote healthy plant growth. Soil care, too, is a vital part of garden maintenance, and digging techniques combined with nutritional treatments are just as important as regular weeding for a well-tended, fertile garden.

Levels and levelling

Changes in level in a garden can be visually attractive but can equally be susceptible to poor drainage, soil erosion and weak plant growth. Installing a soakaway (see page 11) to cope with poor drainage, along with forms of soil improvement (see pages 12–13), can aid the condition but you may find that remodelling the earth is more beneficial.

If the garden is composed of substantial differences in level, work within these contours. But remember that a slope should look as natural as possible. If it lies at an angle steeper than 30 degrees, the nourishing topsoil will be eroded by rainwater and underground water movements may cause sinking.

Cutting and filling

Improving the shape of exisiting levels can be accomplished using the cut-and-fill technique: soil is taken from one high area and used to fill in a low spot.

If a bank appears too steep, first dig out the topsoil to about 150mm (6in) and set it aside for re-use; dig out and save the same depth of topsoil from the low level.

Excavate the subsoil to the required depth and transport it by barrow to the low level. Spread it out over the exposed subsoil, then roll it or tramp over it with the heels of your boots. Replace the topsoil at the top and bottom of the bank.

Level pegging

If you want to build a patio or lay a lawn, you'll need a relatively flat, well-drained area.

Choose a suitable site that won't involve massive restructuring of the ground. Drive a 300 × 25 × 25mm (12 × 1 × 1in) timber peg into the ground with a club hammer, so that its top is set at the required level for the whole plot.

Use this 'prime datum' peg as a guide to sinking more pegs in the ground over the area you're levelling, at about 1.5m (5ft) intervals. All the pegs must be set in the ground at the same level. To check this, place one end of a 1.8m (6ft) long plank on the prime datum peg and the other end on top of the second peg. Place a spirit level on the plank edge and adjust the level of the second peg. When the second peg is level, drive in a third peg and level it with the second. Continue in this way across the site.

Adjust the level of the soil so that it's flush with the top of the pegs. Compact the area lightly to accentuate dips and fill with more soil. If there are voids that cannot be filled by cutting-and-filling, add a few extra barrowloads of soil, obtained from a garden centre. Finally rake over the site to give a flat finish.

Levelling by sight

If the ground to be levelled is very rough, you will not be able to use the peg and plank technique. Instead employ 'boning rods'.

Make up three rods, each 900 × 50 × 25mm (36 × 2 × 1in) softwood with a 300mm (12in) cross-piece nailed at the top, forming a T-shape.

Drive a 300 × 25 × 25mm (12 × 1 × 1in) softwood peg into the ground at the

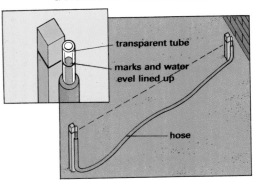

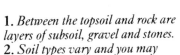

Above *Make a water level from a length of garden hose with a short piece of clear plastic tube in each end. Mark the tube with adhesive tape as a gauge. Stretch the hose between the datum peg and the one you're levelling; fill the hose with water and align the tape marks with the peg tops. Adjust the level of the second peg until the water levels are the same at each end.*

highest point, leaving about 50mm (2in) protruding. Insert a second peg about 600 mm (2ft) away and set it at the same level as the first.

Stand a boning rod upright on each peg and, crouching down, sight across the tops to the third rod held on another peg by a helper at the opposite side of the site. Adjust the third peg until the cross-pieces on all rods are level when sighted across.

Water levels

A third method is to use a water level – working on the principle that water finds its own level. Fit a short piece of clear plastic tube into each end of a long length of garden hose. Wind tape around the clear tube as a guide to levelling. Fill the hose with water and hold one end against a datum peg; get a helper to hold the other end at a second peg. Align the tape marks with the peg tops and adjust the height of the pegs until the water levels are the same at each end.

Better garden drainage

Poor garden drainage is readily identifiable: you'll notice pools of water that linger after heavy rainfall and even on dry days, drenched soil. Plant and shrub growth will be weak, and specimens may suffer attacks of mildew and rotting of the roots. Wet soils are also cold, which retards the growth of plants.

In severe cases, expansion and shrinkage in certain subsoils, as water is absorbed and lost, can actually cause subsidence in the house foundations, or can at least cause cracks to appear in the walls.

Many drainage defects can be remedied simply by improving the soil content naturally with organic additives (see pages 12–13), or by digging techniques (see page 16–17). But where the soil structure is largely impervious clay, or in area troubled

by frequent heavy rainfall, you may have to install artificial drainage.

Testing the drainage

Your priority is to identify the cause of the problem. Dig a hole about 900mm (3ft) deep by a spade's width and examine the soil you remove. Sandy or stony soil usually drains freely, and good, fertile soils composed of 100mm (4in) or more of topsoil over heavier subsoil should also be no problem. Thick, heavy clay, however, drains extremely badly.

Pour some water into the test hole; if it's still there after 48 hours, the drainage is inadequate and needs attention.

You might discover that the hole fills up with water by itself. This indicates a high water table (the level underground to which water standing on the earth's crust rises). The water table, which conforms roughly to the contours of the ground, varies in depth from area to area; it also fluctuates following wet and dry spells. If it rises in winter it can kill the roots of plants by saturation; if it falls in summer, drought can be equally fatal.

The most beneficial level for the water table is about 900mm (3ft) below ground level, serving deep-rooted and shallow-rooted plants alike.

Consult your local authority's survey or to find out if your area has a particularly high water table; if you live on low-lying ground – below sea level near the coast, or in the flood plain of a river valley – the water table may be at ground level. No drainage system will cure the problem.

In less affected areas, you can usually reduce the water table sufficiently by laying land drains. The drain can be, at its simplest, a gravel-filled trench or, more complex, a network of pipes where drainage is extremely poor.

1. *Between the topsoil and rock are layers of subsoil, gravel and stones.*
2. *Soil types vary and you may find a clay soil, which cracks when it dries out and requires artificial drainage.*
3. *A sandy soil, which has a loose texture through which water and nutrients drain rapidly.*
4. *Loamy soil, well-balanced and the ideal growing medium for plants.*

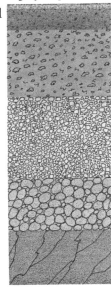

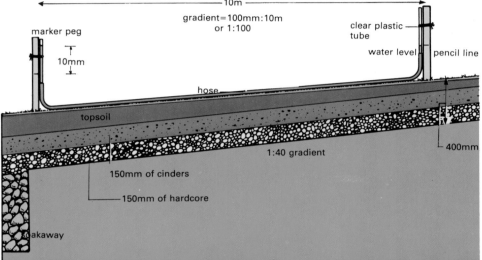

1. *Dig the drainage trench about 300mm (12in) wide and 400mm (16in) deep.*
2. *Tip about 150mm (6in) of hardcore into the trench, add the same amount of cinders, sand or gravel then compact by tramping with your boots.*

Below left *Ensure the drainage trench is set to the correct gradient towards the drainage point using a water level between marker pegs. A gradient of 1:40 is adequate.*

Whatever the type, it must lead to a suitable drainage point: this could be an existing drainage ditch or stream (but beware of draining your garden into a neighbour's!), but most probably a soak-away will need to be constructed. This is basically a rubble-filled pit, which filters the water away.

Measuring the gradient
In a garden that slopes, calculate its approximate gradient before you lay a land drain, so that you can dig your trench to the correct gradient. A gentle consistent slope of 1:40 is adequate; any steeper and water would wash along it, leaving sediment behind which would clog the drain.

You can use the 'water level' method (see page 8) to determine the gradient. Drive a peg into the ground at each end of the garden, with about 300mm (12in) protruding; draw a pencil mark 150mm (6in) from the top of each and run a hosepipe between them, with clear plastic inserts in each end. Tie the hose to the pegs and fill it with water. When the water reaches the line drawn on one end, this is the lower ground;

continue to fill the hose until the water reaches the second line.

Measure how far above the first line the water has now risen and the distance between the two pegs. If, for instance, the pegs are 10m (33ft) apart, and the height difference between the pencil marks is 100mm (4in), you have a gradient of 1:100. Where your garden slopes towards the house, you'll have to dig the drainage trench deeper to avoid the foundations.

Mark out the run of your drainage trench using string stretched between wooden pegs: if the garden slopes away from the house, run the trench towards the lowest point, where there should be a soakaway.

Digging a drainage trench
Start to dig a trench about 300mm (12in) wide along the stringline. If you're laying the drain in a lawn, carefully remove the turf in rectangles about 300 × 450mm (12 × 18in), roll them up (grass inwards) and set aside. Measure the length of the proposed trench and work out how deep it must be at the lowest end: the highest end should be a minimum of 400mm (16in) deep.

Make sure that the trench slopes gradually and consistently to the far end – place a long, straight-edged plank in the bottom of the excavation to check this.

Tip about 150mm (6in) of hardcore (broken bricks or concrete), or coarse gravel mixed with stones, into the base of the trench to act as a water filter. Don't use old gypsum plaster, however, as this will dissolve and clog up the filter. Rubble left over from other DIY building projects, or obtained from a nearby demolition site, is particularly ideal.

Add about 150mm (6in) of cinders, coarse sand or gravel to the hardcore layer then compact both layers lightly, by tramping with your boots, to discourage future subsidence. Return the topsoil to the trench so it stands proud of the surrounding ground; re-lay any turves. The trench will stand out when complete, but will sink back in due course.

Piped drainage

Where inadequate drainage affects the whole garden, you'll need to lay a system of underground pipes running into a soakaway. The most efficient set-up is to lay the pipes in a herring-bone pattern – a central spine leading to the drainage point, with branches fanning from it.

Draw a scale plan of your garden on squared paper and include on it the house, the planned pipe runs and soakaway. Note down the lengths of each section to help you work out how much pipe you'll need. Calculate the gradient of the garden and work out how deep you'll have to dig the trenches. The main spine should slope at a gradient of 1:40 to the soakaway. It's a good idea to clearly mark out the route on site with a series of stringlines.

Pipes are made in a range of materials, plastic, concrete, pitch fibre or unglazed clay. They're either perforated or un-perforated in 75–100mm (3–4in) diameters. Choose the larger size for the central spine, the smaller ones for the branches.

There's little to choose between materials, although pitch fibre can be joined with snap connectors, plastic are made in long runs and can be bent (to avoid obstacles such as tree roots). Clay (known as field pipes), although inexpensive and in 400mm (16in) lengths, can't be cut without an angle grinder – a club hammer and bolster chisel would only shatter the pipe.

Prepare the trenches as previously described then line the base of each with a 50mm (2in) layer of fine gravel. Position the pipes in the trenches, starting with the spine at the lowest level.

Perforated pipes allow surplus water to filter away, so position the perforations towards the bottom. Unperforated pipes must be laid with a 12mm (½in) gap between them to allow the water to flow inside.

Some pipes – particularly pitch fibre or concrete – are porous and allow a little water to seep through their walls.

Extend the spine of the drain about 300mm (12in) into the soakaway pit so there's no danger at all of the water seeping to earth. Then you should lay the branch pipes.

Where you've left gaps between pipes, go back over the run and cover each joint with a roof tile or a small sheet of tough polythene sheeting, to stop earth and gravel clogging the pipes.

Cover the pipes with a further layer of

Below *Set land drainage pipes in the trench, the joins covered with pieces of tile, then cover with coarse gravel to within 150mm (6in) of the ground level. Top with soil or turf. The best arrangement for the system is a herringbone pattern (inset) draining towards a soakaway.*

1. Lay the drain pipes in the trench on a gravel base with a 15mm (½in) gap between them.
2. Cover the joins with polythene sheet or tile then sprinkle gravel on top.
3. Continue the drain run into the centre of the soakaway.
4. Bury the pipes in gravel then add a sheet of glass fibre matting or clay to preventing silting. Fill the soakaway to ground level with topsoil then returf or plant out.

gravel, taking care not to dislodge the polythene or tile covers. Add about 150mm (6in) of topsoil to slightly over-fill the trenches and replace the turves you've previously removed.

Constructing a soakaway

The soakaway is the heart of a garden drainage system. Basically it's a large hole, filled with rubble to filter the water back to earth, and topped with a soil layer that can be cultivated.

The pit should be installed at the lowest part of the garden. Remove any turf or topsoil and set aside for re-use. Mark out the perimeter of the pit with stringlines, then dig down to the required depth: the soakaway should be 900mm (3ft) deep below the level of the incoming drainage pipe, and if you've a very large garden you could find yourself digging down this far any way, before you actually start to dig the drainage pit itself.

Fill the pit with hardcore, rubble and large stones to the level of the drainpipe. Compact the infill well using a sledge hammer (or a fence post – wear thick gloves to avoid splinters). This will reduce the likelihood of subsidence when the aggregate settles.

Now add a layer of coarse gravel or

pebbles to prevent silting, compact this well down then top with about a 150mm (6in) thick layer of clay or if you prefer, a heavy subsoil.

Roll the top layer thoroughly to produce a firm flat surface. You can substitute the clay layer for a sheet of glass fibre matting, as used in loft insulation, or even a thin screed of concrete, to prevent the topsoil filtering down and subsequently clogging the soakaway.

Add topsoil to stand proud of the hole, then re-turf the whole section if necessary, or alternatively, you can plant out the area, if you wish.

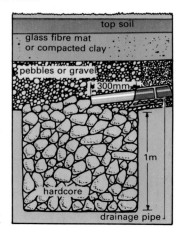

Left The soakaway is basically a deep hole filled with hardcore, which filters water away to earth. The drain pipes should enter the hardcore section, which is then topped with gravel, a layer to stop any silting and then a layer of topsoil.

Improving your soil

Soil is your garden's natural growing medium, so it's vital for the health and successful growth of your plants and crops that you keep it well maintained.

Soil is basically rock that's been ground down by the effects of the weather over a long period of time and made fertile by decayed organic matter (derived from dead insects and leaves). There are hundreds of different soil types, but they can broadly be classified as sandy, loamy or clay, referring to their basic texture.

Texture affects the drainage, aeration and nutrient content of the soil and you may have to take steps to improve on this in certain types of soil.

Which soil type?

Take a handful of soil and run a small amount between your forefinger and thumb. Although all soils contain varying proportions of sand, silt and clay, you'll readily be able to tell the difference between the main types.

Sandy soil feels gritty when dry and even when it's wet particles will not stick together. Loams, on the other hand, can be moulded in the hand when moist, but aren't at all sticky and gritty and are fairly loose when dry. Clay soils are sticky and smooth when wet, but become polished when rubbed and baked hard when dry.

A loamy soil is a well-balanced amalgamation of sand, silt and clay, which combines excellent drainage with sufficient moisture retention to assure good growing conditions for most plants. It's fairly easy to look after, although part-loamy soils do benefit from regular applications of well-

rotted organic matter to prevent compaction.

The particle consistency of sandy soil doesn't hold water well, with the result that plant foods are often taken away by rain before they can do any good. Again well-rotted organic matter can be added to bind the soil particles together.

Clay soils are the most difficult to work, usually becoming waterlogged, when they're virtually impossible to dig. Artificial drainage (see page 8–9) will probably be the first step in improving the texture of the soil and various additives will break down the structure to make use of its excellent food stocks.

Improving soil texture

There are various methods of improving your soil's texture. Essentially this requires regular applications of a well-rotted organic substance called humus, which is obtained from decayed plant and animal matter (manure, compost and seaweed each provide ample sources).

You can identify the humus content of the soil by looking at the colour: the light soils are low in organic content; whitish, sandy soils are extremely poor; the darkest, almost black soils are rich and nutritious.

Humus can be dug in to break up clay soils into a much more open texture, with the benefit of introducing nutrients essential to plant growth. Drainage will be improved also; roots able to penetrate the soil structure rather than following the cracks in the ground. Sandy soils will benefit by being bulked-up by humus-forming materials, whereas materials added to loamy soils will help to retain its existing open texture.

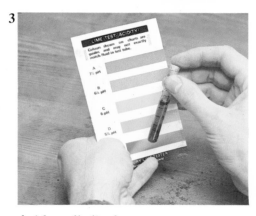

Above *A compost heap is an excellent way to produce your own bulky organic matter from materials you would otherwise dispose of.*

1. *Test the pH value of your soil using a soil-testing kit. Fill one tube quarter full of soil and the other half full of test solution.*
2. *Pour the solution into the tube with the soil in it, then cork and shake it.*
3. *Allow the soil to settle then compare the colour in the tube with the colours on the card.*

Acid or alkaline?

The presence of chalk in soil can also affect the growth of plants: some prefer slightly acid (chalk-free) soils, while others grow more successfully in alkaline, chalky soils. Most fruit and vegetables, however, grow better in neutral soil.

Although benefitting the soil in some ways, compost, manure and fertilizers (see page 12–15) can actually add to its acidity, as organisms break them down.

You can find out the degree of acidity or alkalinity in your soil by testing its pH value, using a soil-testing kit available from garden centres. A typical soil testing kit consists of two test-tubes, chemicals for estimating the acidity of the sample and a colour chart, which indicates the various pH values.

Over-acid soils can be treated with applications of lime – either hydrated (slaked) lime, or ground limestone (chalk). Of the two, ground limestone is your best choice. It may be slow acting but does permit the number of useful soil organisms to increase gradually and won't exhaust organic matter too rapidly. Hydrated lime, although quicker acting, is caustic and mustn't be allowed to blow onto crops or plants or it will burn them.

To apply lime, sprinkle on the broken topsoil and mix in lightly but don't dig in; leave to wash down by rain. Apply lime every other year if need be.

An alkaline soil can be treated with manure, garden compost or peat, well dug in.

Composts and composting

Bulky organic animal manures can be quite difficult to obtain for use in soil improvement but garden compost is an excellent substitute. You can make it yourself from waste vegetable matter from the kitchen or garden. A compost heap costs virtually nothing to make and it recycles nutrients from materials that you would otherwise burn or dispose of.

The waste material is broken down by bacteria and other micro-organisms. For them to thrive and multiply, there must be sufficient airflow through the heap to supply the oxygen they need and to remove the waste carbon dioxide they expel.

There must be enough moisture, nitrogen and non-acidic conditions present for successful composting. High temperatures within the heap, peaking at about 60°C (140°F), are also vital to produce wholesome compost – and to destroy any weed seeds present.

What to compost

For the best compost, use soft waste: lawn mowings, dead leaves, spent lettuces, stems of flowers and crops – even bonfire ashes – are ideal. Avoid woody stems, evergreen leaves and bark, which won't rot down rapidly enough.

You can add weeds to the heap, so long as you place them centrally, where the heat will destroy them and their seeds. However, don't use perennial weeds like couch grass or bindweed, or obviously diseased plants (you may spread the blight through the garden with the compost).

Some kitchen waste makes a good addition to the compost heap. Vegetable trimmings such as cabbage leaves, potato peelings, and fruit waste are all suitable. Crushed egg shells are a good source of calcium, even though they don't rot down, and tea leaves and coffee grounds are beneficial.

Never use cooked scraps, animal wastes, cheese rinds, bones or fat. Not only will they smell foul but also they'll attract vermin and flies.

Aim to make your compost heap up to its required size as quickly as is possible, between the early spring and late summer, so it will have ample time to heat up, rot and be ready for full use in about three months.

Types of compost heap

If you have space, you'll achieve rapid results from a heap measuring about 2 × 2 × 1.5m (6 × 6 × 5ft) high, but in a suburban garden where space will be limited (and materials scarce in sufficiency) it is more realistic to aim for a heap measuring a minimum of about 1.5m (5ft) square, buy a proprietary compost bin, or make an open-topped compost box.

Ready-made containers may be wire-meshed boxes with hinged access panels, or strong black polythene sacks in simple cradles.

A home-made compost bin can be a timber box, slatted for aeration or a breezeblock or corrugated iron structure.

Constructing the heap

To make a compost heap, whether it's open or enclosed, prepare the base by lightly forking the ground: this allows earthworms to gain access to the heap.

Spread a layer of woody prunings over the soil to act as an aeration layer then mix up garden and kitchen waste on the ground nearby. Moisten the mix with a little water and fork into the container (or make a 300mm/12in base layer for an open heap) then compact it lightly with the back of a spade, or tread it in carefully.

If you're making the heap in autumn or winter, pour a thin layer of a nitrogen-rich activator, such as poultry manure, blood or fish meal over the waste to feed the micro-organisms inside.

Add another layer of waste. If your soil is

1. Make a compost container from preservative-treated planks nailed to vertical posts set in the ground.
2. Ensure an airflow through the heap by containing it within a circle of wire netting, plasticized to prevent rust.
3. One of the simplest containers is a tough black plastic sack set in a simple cradle made from old piping or timber. Puncture the sack to ensure air reaches the compost.
4. Breezeblocks built up without mortar, make a sturdy compost container. Support it within timber posts and raise it on bricks to ensure airflow.
5. Corrugated plastic sheeting held by timber posts makes a lightweight compost container, and you can allow separate sections for material in use and that in production. Lay drainpipes on the ground to introduce air to the centre of the heap.

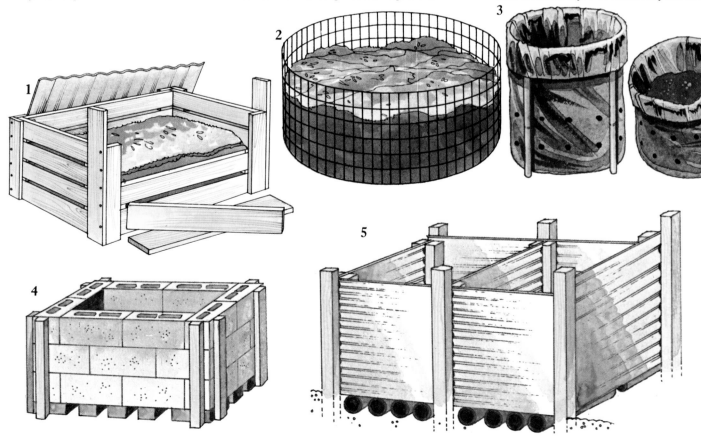

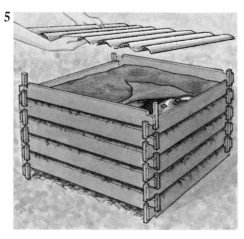

1. *Fork the ground to allow beneficial earthworms to enter the heap.*
2. *Build your container (if necessary) then add an aeration layer followed by a mix of kitchen and garden waste.*
3. *Pour a little activator such as poultry manure on the waste.*
4. *Add a second layer of waste and sprinkle on ground limestone if the soil is strongly acid to maintain the correct pH.*
5. *Build the heap in these layers to fill the container, cover with punctured black polythylene and a piece of sacking or carpet, then add the lid.*
6. *Examine the material after about three months; it should be dark brown and crumbly when ready for use.*

strongly acid, sprinkle ground limestone on top of the second layer to maintain the heap at the correct pH – you'll need about 120g per sq m (4oz per sq yd). Top the limestone with a layer of wood ashes or soil, about 2.4kg per sq m (5lb per sq yd), to ensure that any ammonia gas doesn't escape before the micro-organisms in the heap can use it.

Continue to build up the heap in these layers until you have filled the container (or slope an open heap up and inwards).

Spread a sheet of punctured black polythene over the heap, then cover with sacking or an old carpet, followed by the lid.

The heap should heat up to about 60°C (140°F) within seven days and after another week the material should have shrunk to about one-third of its height. Top up the heap at this stage.

Turning the heap isn't necessary if it's well insulated, although after about six weeks you should fork the cooler outsides into the warm centre.

When the heap cools you may notice red

manure worms inside: these are vital to convert the compost into fine crumbs. Once the heap is cooled it will start to mature. Investigate the material after about three to four months; it should be dark brown and crumbly if it's ready for use.

Digging

Digging is an essential part of improving the quality of your soil. Not only does it enable you to incorporate organic matter, such as manure and compost, well down into the soil structure, but also it will break up hard layers of soil (called pans) lower down. These pans are often caused by cultivation of the soil to the same depth over a number of years.

Choosing and using tools

Buy the best spade and fork you can afford. Choose a spade with a stainless steel blade (which won't rust) with either a wood or alloy handle in a weight that suits you; the blade should be full-sized – 300 × 200mm (12 × 8in). A fork should have four

Single digging

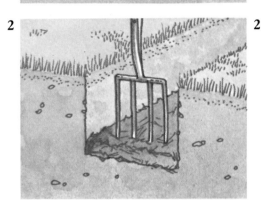

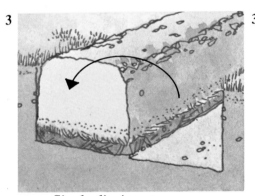

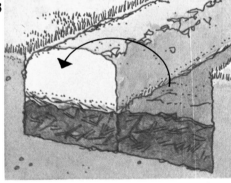

Half trenching

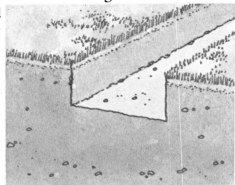

Single digging

1. *Dig a trench about 300mm (12in) deep and wide, across one end of the plot or strip.*
2. *Add some organic matter to the trench and fork it into the soil, then rake it level.*
3. *Dig a second trench parallel to the first, turning the forkful of soil into the first trench.*

Half trenching

1. *Dig a spit-deep trench 600mm (24in) wide, and transfer the soil to the other end of the plot.*
2. *Loosen the subsoil a spit deep with your fork them mix in some organic matter.*
3. *Dig a second trench, parallel to the first, and toss the earth into the first trench.*

cylindrical prongs for normal work, or square tines for breaking up hard ground.

To use a spade or fork correctly, place your right hand on the handle and your left hand on the shaft, near the handle (vice versa if you're left-handed), then insert the blade or tines perfectly upright to their full depth.

Press down with your left foot. Pull back the handle, sliding your left hand down the shaft to take the weight of the soil. Lift and tip where required.

Methods of digging

There are basically four methods of digging: single digging, half (or bastard) trenching, full trenching (double digging) and ridging.

Single digging should be carried out each autumn. Its purpose is to turn over a spade-ful or forkful of soil – what's called a 'spit' or spade's depth – leaving it rough and

burying any annual weeds.

If you have a large plot, divide the area into strips with stringlines and pegs. Dig a trench about 250mm deep and 300mm wide (10 × 12in), across one end of the plot or strip. Transfer the soil by barrow to the opposite end of the plot.

If you want to add organic matter to the soil, fork it into the base of the trench and rake it.

Start to dig a second trench, about 150mm (6in) away from the first. Insert your spade or fork to its full depth, lever out a block of soil and toss it forward into the first trench, turning it completely over. Repeat this action across the strip, not forgetting to add manure or compost to each trench.

Continue down the strip, up the next and so on to the end of the plot. Shovel the soil you removed from the first trench into the last.

Half trenching is especially beneficial to heavy, or badly drained soils, and should be carried out every third year to break up a hard pan.

Divide your plot into equal strips then dig out a spit-deep trench 600mm (2ft) wide; transfer the soil to the end of the plot.

Use a fork to loosen the subsoil in the bottom of the trench a spit-deep. Incorporate organic matter with the subsoil. Step back and dig out another spade-deep trench 600mm (2ft) wide and toss (and invert) the block of earth forward into the first trench. You'll find it easier to remove these blocks in two halves, as full width ones are heavy.

Repeat this procedure to the end of the plot and fill the final trench with your barrowload of earth from the first trench.

Full trenching, or double digging, improves badly-drained soil and prepares the ground for planting permanent crops.

Divide the plot into strips, dig a trench 250 × 900mm (10 × 36in) and take the soil to the end of the plot. Divide the trench in half along its length with a stringline and dig out soil from the front half to 250mm (10in) deep. Remove this soil to the final trench position but don't mix it with the first heap.

Back at the first, deeper trench, fork the base to 250mm (10in) deep and add manure. Dig spit-deep blocks from the rear half of the original trench, and turn them over onto the broken up front half. Fork the base of the rear half of the trench to 250mm (10in) and add manure.

Mark out a 450mm (18in) wide strip and dig out the topsoil to 250mm (10in) deep. Toss this onto the 'step' in the front half of the original trench.

Dig down another 250mm (10in) and throw the blocks of soil onto the broken up soil of the rear half of the original trench.

Continue in this way across the plot. Add the smaller heap of soil taken from the low part of the first trench to the base of the last one and fill it with the larger heap of topsoil.

Ridging exposes a large area of soil to the weather. Divide your plot into 900mm (3ft) wide strips with string and pegs.

Start at one end of the first strip and remove a trench 300mm wide × 250mm deep (12 × 10in) across it.

Work down the length of the strip, single digging in 300 × 250mm (12 × 10in) deep blocks. Throw the soil blocks from the left-hand side in towards the centre of the strip; throw the blocks from the centre spit forwards; and the blocks from the right-hand spit in towards the centre.

Repeat for the next 900mm (3ft) wide strip and so on across the plot, forming a series of steep-sided ridges.

No-digging

Some gardeners prescribe to the 'no-digging' school of thought. In this method the soil surface is permanently covered with organic matter – often compost.

The unbroken soil below has many tiny cracks and channels, caused by worms and plant roots can easily penetrate these. Ideally, the channels allow good drainage and aeration of the soil, which aids root growth. Digging, despite its benefits, destroys these channels.

The organic layer retains moisture, smothers weeds and is taken down and released at lower levels by worms. It encourages the roots of crops to grow in an undisturbed manner at the top 50mm (2in) of soil.

Full trenching

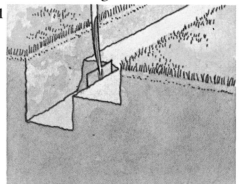

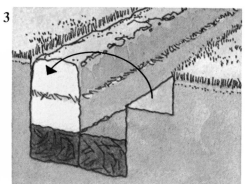

Full trenching

1. *Dig a trench 250mm deep × 900mm wide (10in × 3ft), divide the trench in half, dig one half a spit deep.*
2. *Add organic matter to the first half, dig the second half a spit deep and turn the soil onto the first half.*
3. *Add organic matter to the second half, dig a second trench 250mm (10in) deep, turning it onto the first half of the first trench.*
4. *Dig down another 250mm (10in) and turn the earth onto the second half of the first trench.*

Ridging

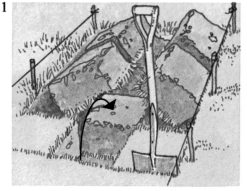

Ridging

1. *Divide the plot into 900mm (3ft) wide strips; work down the strip digging 300mm (12in) wide × 250mm (10in) deep blocks. Turn the blocks from the left-hand side into the centre, those from the centre, forwards, and those from the right-hand side towards the centre.*
2. *Repeat this procedure for subsequent 900mm (3ft) wide strips, forming steep-sided ridges.*

1. *Sprinkle fertilizer over the entire area you want to treat.*
2. *Rake it into the top 75mm (3in) of ground.*

Right *A graphic demonstration of how nutrient deficiency affects plant growth: both tomato plants were started at the same time but the plant on the left was starved of nourishment, whereas the plant on the right was treated with force fertilizer, producing a well-proportioned, are generally much more healthy plant.*

Fertilizers

Plants need a plentiful supply of nutrients to remain healthy, but the natural plant foods in the soil are constantly being leached away or used up in growth. Bulky organic matter such as manure, used to condition the soil supplies some nutrients, but you will probably need to add more, in the form of fertilizer, to sustain vigorous growth.

Fertilizers are concentrated forms of chemical salts, absorbed by the plant roots to sustain growth. Whether the nutrients come from a natural organic source or from a manufactured product matters little to the plant. But it is important to realize that fertilizers are no substitute for manures and other bulky organic materials such as garden compost. Manure improves the structure and physical characteristics of the soil as well as providing some nutrients. Fertilizers and manures should be working together.

Plants require numerous chemical nutrients, notably nitrogen, phosphorus, and potassium. These elements influence the growth and development of plants but must be administered in the correct proportions.

The effects of nutrients

Nitrogen is essential to plant growth, especially leaf growth; phosphorus (absorbed in the form of phosphates) is important for root crops, seedlings, potassium is particularly useful for flower and fruit production.

A lack of nitrogen will result in spindly, weak growth with small, pale green or yellow leaves; too much will produce over-vigorous growth. Phosphorus deficiency is

similar to that of nitrogen, with scorched leaf margins; premature ripening of the plant signals an overdose of the element. Scorching of the leaf margins is indicative of low potassium reserves; plants may be bushy but any fruit will be small and woody.

It is important to realize, however, that these are very generalized symptoms and the subject is more complex than can be dealt with here. Some of these symptoms may be due to other causes.

Other essential chemicals are often present in the soil in the right quantity. 'Trace' elements, including sodium, iron, and magnesium, are needed in only tiny amounts, and you should not attempt to add these as individual elements unless you know that there is a deficiency (which may need expert diagnosis).

The amount of fertilizer needed can be affected by many things, including the type of soil, but you won't go far wrong if you follow the guidance on the packet or bottle.

Sources of fertilizer

Each of the nutrients can be obtained separately, or in various proprietary combinations. The maze of different fertilizer elements is vast. Organic sources of nitrogen, mainly derived from dead animals, include dried blood and hoof and horn meal; inorganic sources, which are less expensive, are typified by sulphate of ammonia, Nitro-chalk, nitrate of ammonia and nitrate of soda.

Phosphatic fertilizers include organic bonemeal (with calcium phosphate as its active ingredient) and inorganic super-phosphate of lime, and basic slag.

Potassium is available in the form of potash. Wood ashes and sulphate of potash are good sources of the nutrient.

This list is by no means exhaustive, the choice of fertilizers being allied strictly to your soil's particular requirements. Although single-element fertilizers such as these are the most economical to buy, combined types can enable all the necessary plant foods to be supplied in a single application. The three main types are:
● **General fertilizers** These consist of nitrogen, phosphorus, and potash.
● **Complete fertilizers** Rather like general types, they also contain trace elements as well as the three main nutrients.
● **Compound fertilizers** These are made up of two or more plant nutrients in a single chemical combination.

Mixing your own fertilizers

By purchasing single-element fertilizers, you can mix them yourself to make your own compound types. You must not combine substances that will cause an unfavourable

Left *Nitrogenous fertilizer is applied in a ring around each plant.*

Below left *Apply liquid fertilizer by a watering-can fitted with a fine rose.*

reaction, however – some types will produce harmful acids if mixed and these could be harmful to the soil.

When proportioning the ingredients of your combined fertilizer, all quantities must be measured in multiples of the same basic unit of weight. To discover what the basic unit should be for your plot, muiltiply the area of the plot by the rate of application, then divide this figure by the total number of parts in the mix.

As an illustration of this, a general fertilizer (a top-dressing for vegetables or an additive prior to sowing or planting) consists of 5 parts sulphate of ammonia: 7 parts superphosphate: 2 parts sulphate of potash: 1 part steamed boneflour. It should be applied at the rate of 90g per sq m (3oz per sq yd).

If your plot measures 30sq m (30sq yd) the total amount of fertilizer is $30 \times 90g = 2700g$ ($30 \times 3oz = 90oz$). Divide this by the total number of parts in the mix (15) to arrive at $2700 \div 15 = 180g$ ($90 \div 15 = 6oz$). Your basic unit, therefore, is 180g (6oz).

Now multiply each part of the mix by the basic unit to arrive at the amounts of each ingredient you'll need:
- sulphate of ammonia = 900g (30oz)
- superphosphate = 1260g (42oz)
- sulphate of potash = 360g (12oz)
- steamed boneflour = 180g (6oz)

When mixing, make sure all the ingredients are kept perfectly dry. Use only clean tools, containers, surfaces and bags.

Ensure that all the ingredients are thoroughly blended. Place the ingredients on a large clean and flat board in layers. Shovel out a segment of the 'sandwich' and mix it thoroughly on another board. Repeat this procedure until you've used up the pile.

Liquid fertilizers

General fertilizers can also be bought in liquid form. The liquid is diluted with water and applied by watering-can (with a fine rose) or as a 'foliar' (leaf) treatment via a garden sprayer. The latter method ensures rapid absorption of the nutrients, but is more time-consuming to apply.

Applying dry fertilizers

Fertilizers can be applied to the soil prior to sowing or planting, or later as a top-dressing around plants. Scatter the material over the soil evenly, then rake into the top-soil and water in if necessary.

CHAPTER 2

GARDEN MATERIALS

Every garden must have its basic structure to tie together the various aspects of the plot. This framework may be composed of a number of versatile materials to give the pracitcal or decorative effect you want for your style of garden.

Opposite A selection of the bricks that can be used in the garden for a host of structures from garden boundary walls, retaining walls and decorative structures.

Below Cloches can be made from a variety of materials such as polythene sheeting on a wire frame, rigid PVC held together with clips, and glass, again secured in a basic wire frame.

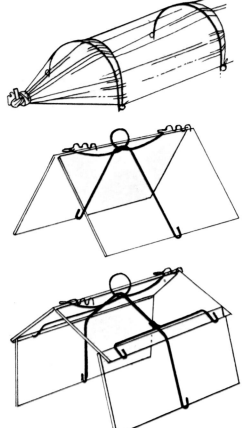

There is so much more to a garden than flower beds, a lawn and vegetable patch. Even the plainest, most compact plot is built around a framework of walls and fences, to form boundaries or to divide various areas, paths to give access through the garden, and steps in a sloping site.

Embellishing the basic skeleton, there are decorative touches such as pergolas and trellises, patterned, textured surfaces for the patio, and the functional structures – cold frames and a greenhouse for raising plants, a shed for storage and a summerhouse for relaxation.

The materials used to construct all these different items range from durable concrete, versatile brick and stone, to the beauty of timber and the efficiency of glass and plastic. Each needs to be chosen with care to suit your type of garden, and needs to be regularly maintained to keep everything in prime condition and looking good.

Glass and plastic

Glass plays an important role in the garden. It is still the most widely used glazing material for greenhouses, and on a smaller scale, it is used to make cold frames and cloches to protect or force plants. Glass is better than plastic for greenhouses and cloches because it lets the sun's heat pass through, then retains it; plastic lets heat through, too, but once the sun sinks, the greenhouse cools rapidly – not ideal for healthy plants. Glass has limitations, however, because it is fragile; lightweight, durable plastics are now popular as a substitute. Plastics can also be moulded to make anything from plant labels to garden tools, equipment and accessories.

Glass and where to use it

Modern production methods produce flat, flawless sheets of glass, but such fine quality isn't necessary in the garden. So long as the glass is reasonably free from bubbles, which can concentrate the sun's burning rays onto plants, slight kinks won't have an adverse affect.

Horticultural glass is about half the price

of float glass, so it is sensible to buy this if you need a replacement. You can, however, make use of any glass you have at home: an old window frame for instance, makes an exceedingly good cold frame when mounted on bricks.

Plastic and its uses

Plastic is available in numerous forms, from rigid PVC, used in sheet form for greenhouse panes and cloches (some proprietary cloches with spikes to stick into the ground are made from this material) to polythene sheeting, which is either flexible (in rolls) or rigid (in sheets). In its transparent form it can be used to clad a greenhouse with an insulating layer in winter, or in opaque black it can be used as a mulch round plants.

Where strength is needed, choose plastic sheeting reinforced with strong plastic or wire mesh, or rigid corrugated PVC sheets, which make an excellent substitute for greenhouse glass. Remember: plastic for glazing must be transparent, not coloured or tinted.

Some polythene will become brittle and can lose its transparency after about three years' exposure to the ultra-violet rays in sunlight (although a horticultural grade is made, which delays this reaction). Also, because the surface is soft, wind-blown particles can scratch it. In its favour, it is cheap to renew.

Shading for plants

On really hot days greenhouse plants need shading to prevent scorching: the cheapest method is to paint a diluted concentrate of electrostatic paint onto the outside of the greenhouse or cold frame. The paint is waterproof, but can be wiped off easily when dry. If you think this too messy, interior roller blinds with translucent PVC sheeting give adjustable shade. You can make one yourself using a roller blind kit and a sheet of tinted plastic.

Reglazing a greenhouse

Despite its flimsy nature, a greenhouse will repel most onslaughts of weather, but it will

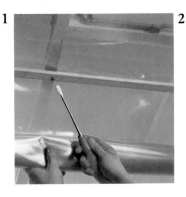
1

2

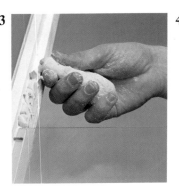
3

4

1. Transparent polythene sheeting acts as an effective double glazing during cold winter spells.
2. Carefully remove a cracked pane with thick gloves, and clean and repaint the rebate before you reglaze.
3. Apply putty into the clean rebates pressing it into place with your thumb. Position the new pane.
4. Secure the new pane with metal glazing sprigs, sliding the hammer across the glass. Trim off excess putty.

be lucky to escape a direct hit – from a stray football or a fallen branch. But repairing a smashed pane is quite easy.

First measure the dimensions of the pane. In most greenhouses the higher panes overlap the ones below, so rainwater runs off; add an extra 9mm (³⁄₈in) to top and bottom for this. On timber-framed greenhouses the glass is usually located in rebates, bedded in a layer of putty and secured with glazing sprigs or headless brass or galvanized pins. Put on a pair of thick gloves to protect your hands and remove the broken glass.

Scrape off the old putty and prise out the pins with a pair of pincers. Sand down the rebates then repaint with white lead paint. Apply new linseed oil putty, pressing it in with your thumb. Position the replacement pane on the putty and press down evenly at the edges.

Secure by tapping new sprigs or pins into the side of the rebate under the bottom overlap (special S-shaped clips are also made). Add more pins at each side of the glass then trim off the surplus putty with a putty knife.

On aluminium-framed houses, the panes are held in the rebates on neoprene or foam rubber seal with metal clips, which can just be refixed to the new pane and carefully reinserted.

Double glazing
Although efficient greenhouse heaters are available, during a really hard winter it is wise to take steps to reduce heat loss through the glass (more so on a plastic-clad house). Here's where glass and plastic complement each other: polythene sheeting fixed firmly to the greenhouse frame, directly under the glass, makes an excellent and economical insulator.

On a timber frame, unroll some material and starting at the apex of the roof, sandwich the sheet between 25mm × 10mm (1in × ³⁄₈in) softwood battens fixed horizontally across the underside of the glazing bars. Fix the battens with 19mm (³⁄₄in) panel pins. Space the battens about 600mm (2ft) apart.

Paving
Pre-cast concrete slabs greatly simplify the job of laying a paved area, and because they're available in numerous sizes, colours, shapes and textures, there is plenty of scope for planning a decorative surface. Small-scale clay paving bricks and concrete block pavers are also available for a more intricately-patterned surface.

Hardwearing and durable, slabs and pavers are easy to lay on a sand bed over firm foundations. You can use mortar to stick the units down, although some blocks (known as 'flexible pavers') are especially made for dry-laying.

Prepare a level, flat site, incorporating the necessary drainage crossfall (see pages 9–11), using pegs and a spirit-level. To prevent the paving wandering you should install edge restraints at the perimeter of the site: these can be pre-cast concrete kerbstones (in plain or wavy designs), bricks on edge, or even preservative-treated timber. If the paving abuts a wall, this can serve as the restraint.

Dig a slim trench around the proposed paved area and set the kerbstones or bricks in a 25mm (1in) thick layer of concrete; make sure they're set level or nail timber restraints to pegs. Tip loads of sand onto the foundations and rake to a consistent level about 50mm (2in) thick.

Laying concrete slabs
Concrete slabs can be laid directly on the sand bed (or bedded in fairly stiff mortar if the paved area is to be used for heavy traffic, such as a drive). Stretch a stringline across the site to align the first row of slabs, then trowel five dabs of mortar onto the sand – one at each corner of the slab; one centrally.

Lower the slab onto the mortar. Shuffle it down gently by standing on it and shifting your weight from one foot to the other, until it's well settled, or tap it gently with the handle of your club hammer. If you are laying the slabs dry, simply place them and bed them down.

Continue laying slabs to your stringline,

1. *Mark out the area you're going to pave with strings and pegs then dig out the base to firm, level ground.*
2. *Add a layer of hardcore (broken bricks or concrete) to the base and compact it using a fence post.*
3. *Spread a layer of sand over the hardcore and rake it to about 50mm (2in) thick.*
4. *Lay the bricks on the sand, making sure that they are evenly spaced. Tap them down and fill in between bricks.*
5. *Position the paving slabs on the sand bed on five dabs of mortar then bed them down by stamping.*
6. *Lay crazy paving in the same way but point between the joints with a fairly wet mortar mix.*

leaving 15mm (⅝in) spaces between the slabs as spacers. Place a spirit-level across the slabs to check that they're bedded evenly and gently tap them into place with the hammer handle. If a slab sinks too low, raise it, pack out underneath with more sand, then re-bed it.

Crazy paving

Crazy paving, made from broken concrete slabs, can give a random-patterned effect but does require careful planning to ensure a successful finish. Aim to fit the large, flat-edged stones at the edges or perimeter of the area, then fill in with medium-sized irregular stones and add small pieces to the spaces between.

Lay crazy paving in the same way as other paving, then point in the gaps – these shouldn't be wider than about 50mm (2in) – using a wet mortar mix. Trowel in the mortar, taking care not to smear the surface of the stones.

Laying pavers

Pavers can be laid in numerous patterns, typically herringbone and woven arrangements (see diagrams). Some can be laid on

Right *A selection of attractive patterns which can be created using brick pavers:*
1. *Herringbone*
2. *Basketweave*
3. *Parquet*
4. *Running bond*

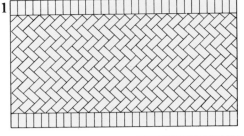

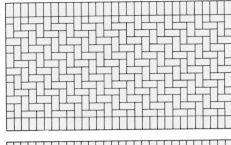

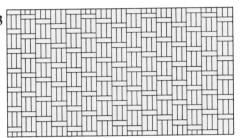

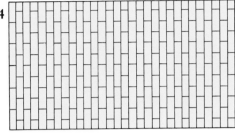

1. *To cut a paving slab, scribe a cutting line across the face using a bolster chisel held against a straightedge length of timber.*
2. *Chop a groove along the line, rest it on the batten aligned with the groove, then break the slab by hitting it with a club hammer.*

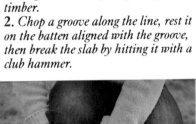

edge, while others have a bevelled top edge to give a neat, recessed joint.

Simply arrange the pavers in your chosen pattern on the sand bed, in a manageable area (if you have to stand on the base, spread your weight with a plank or board). Leave 2–3mm (about 1/6in) gaps between each.

Place a stout length of timber diagonally across the pavers and tap along its length with the club hammer to bed the units down evenly. Check with a spirit level that they're laid correctly, then proceed on to the next area.

Cutting slabs or pavers
You will have to cut some slabs or pavers to fit at the edges: do this by hand using a club hammer and bolster chisel, or else hire a hydraulic stone splitter (see pages 68–71), which gives the cleanest cut.

To cut a slab by hand, scribe a cutting line all the way round it using a chisel, chop a groove along the line then, with the slab resting on a length of wood, aligned with the groove, tap it with a hammer handle to snap it. Do the same for cutting pavers, but after scoring, strike the chisel sharply to split it.

For very large areas of paving it is necessary to compact the units well into the sand bed, to prevent subsidence. To do this you'll need to hire a motorized plate compactor (see pages 68–71), fitted with a rubber sole plate so you don't scuff the pavers. Run over the paving with the machine to bed the units down evenly.

Filling the gaps
Once you've laid all the paving – slabs or pavers – you can fill the gaps between units. There are various ways to do this. Flexible pavers, for example, only require sand to be brushed into their joints and the surface

vibrated with a plate compactor.

Gaps between other types of paving (some slabs, and bricks for example) can be filled with dry mortar brushed in, then watered from the fine rose of a watering-can. For a really firm finish, however, point with a bricklaying mortar mix of 1 part cement to four parts soft sand, trowelled into every gap. It's a laborious, time-consuming job, but does give permanent, rigid, weed-proof joints.

Paving repairs
If the ground beneath a paved area sinks, slabs or pavers are likely to break unless they are supported evenly. Remove a broken slab or paver by levering it up. If the ground is soft, ram pieces of hardcore into the dip then top with sand to just over the level of the surrounding base. Place a new matching stone and tap it down with a club hammer over a block of wood. On a driveway it is best to fit a replacement slab on a complete bed of strong mortar mix (1 part masonry cement, three parts soft sand).

Wood in the garden
Wood is used extensively in the garden for its structural strength and decorative qualities. Whether it's for fences, sheds, greenhouses, frames for climbing plants, steps or pergolas, there's one common factor that is always a problem – the weather.

Wood in its 'manufactured' state needs regular attention to prevent deterioration. Identifying the type of wood and understanding its particular qualities will help you to care for it properly.

Types of wood
Although wood is cut from many varieties of trees, it can be divided into two main groups – softwoods and hardwoods. The

terms describe the type of tree from which the wood was cut, not its hardness (although generally hardwoods *are* harder than softwoods). Softwoods come from coniferous (cone-bearing) trees such as pine, larch and fir; hardwoods come from trees with broad leaves, such as oak and beech. Hardwoods, quite scarce and expensive, are usually reserved for jobs that require a superior finish and are rarely used in garden constructions.

Softwoods are economical and easy to saw, plane and sand, and they hold screws well, although nails can cause splitting along the grain. There are many different species of softwoods but the main ones are pine, redwood or deal.

Buying timber

Softwood is sold in a vast range of lengths and sections, either 'sawn' or 'planed'. Sawn is cheaper than planed and generally used where a smooth appearance isn't necessary: most outdoor projects fall into this category. Planed timber (commonly known by the abbreviation PAR – planed all round) is sold by its nominal planed size; the actual size is about 3mm (1/8in) less all the way round.

Timber is prepared at the sawmill in metric lengths, but many timber merchants sell it in units of 300mm (the 'metric foot'), which actually measures 11¾in. Beware when ordering: if you ask for 'six feet of timber' you may be given a piece 6 *metric* feet long – this is only 1.8m (5ft 10½in) long. If you really do want the full 6ft (1.83m) you will probably have to buy 7 metric feet (2.1m/6ft 6in) and then waste the surplus.

Consult the chart below for the full range of timber sizes that are available.

Above *Wood that is going to be used outside must first be treated with preservative. This is easy to do yourself and it does not take too long to apply.*

Treating wood

Most softwood used outdoors must be treated with preservative to protect it against decay and insect attack. The exception is Western red cedar, which weathers to an attractive silver-grey.

You can buy pre-treated wood from some timber merchants, which has been pressure-injected with a fluid that wards against fungal and insect attack. It is expensive, and treating the wood yourself with one of the many proprietary fluids is an appealing idea, even if the results may not be as good.

Creosote is the traditional preservative. Based on oil and tar, it stains the wood a

Sawn and planed timber sizes

thickness mm	12.5	16	19	25	32	38	50	75	100	125	150	175	200	225	300	thickness in
12.5	■			■		■	■	■	■		■					½
16		■		■		■	■									⅝
19			■	■		■	■	■	■		■	■		■	■	¾
25				■		■	■	■	■	■	■	■	■	■	■	1
32					■		■	■	■		■	■		■	■	1¼
38						■	■	■	■		■			■	■	1½
50							■	■	■		■	□	□	■	□	2
75								■	■		■	□	□	■		3
100									■				□	■	■	4
	⅝	¾	1	1¼	1½	2	3	4	5	6	7	8	9	12		width

Key
■ = Available sawn or planed
□ = Available sawn only

Some of the common defects you may find when buying timber. Look out for twists and warps (1) by peering down its length; shakes (2), which are splits along the grain of the timber; knots (3), which may be loose, fall out and be difficult to cut through; Live knots may ooze resin; discoloration (4), which won't affect your choice if you're painting or creosoting the timber.

dark tone, which you may consider unattractive. Additionally, the protective effect only lasts about two years.

Solvent-based preservatives, although often more costly than creosote, offer more efficient, longer-lasting protection. There's also a selection of wood shades to choose from (and even a clear fluid, if you'd rather not alter the colour). Most preservatives, unlike creosote, can be overpainted if preferred.

The protection given by any preservative relies on thorough penetration of the wood fibres. Apply the fluid generously by brush, making sure you treat all sides equally. Apply at least two coats. The cut ends of timber, which expose the absorbent end grain, are most vulnerable, so apply more coats to these parts. Better still, stand the wood in a container of fluid and leave it to soak in for a few days, periodically brushing the fluid up the sides. Invert the wood and leave for another few days to ensure thorough soaking.

Faults in timber

Timber can suffer from a number of defects, mainly caused by too rapid or uneven drying during 'seasoning' (the process in which the moisture and sap contents are reduced for easier workability and rot resistence). Examine each piece and reject any that suffers from excessive knots (either oozing resin or dried up and loose), which make the wood difficult to saw and can fall out, warping across or along the grain; shakes, which are splits between the annular rings, or along the grain.

Using timber outdoors

Armed with a good sharp saw, a hammer and a screwdriver, there's no reason why you can't construct a variety of timber structures around the garden – anything from a basic formwork box for casting concrete, to a shed, fence or pergola. Study made-up examples and work out how they're put together, then buy your own materials and set to work.

Bear in mind the following points when erecting timber frames:

● Support the posts, for a pergola, for instance, on non-rusting metal fittings, which have a channel or socket into which the post can be bolted, and held above the ground. The metal support is bedded in concrete.
● Prevent the passage of any damp to the wood by setting posts and other components on bituminous felt. Secure the frames with metal dowels set in the concrete and driven through its end.

Types of fencing

There are numerous types of fences, and which you choose to make or erect depends on whether you want a sturdy boundary for your garden, a windbreak around a patio, or just a decorative way to define the vegetable plot, lawn and flower beds.

Closeboard fences are the most common type. Solid and durable, they make excellent garden boundaries. Vertical overlapping boards are nailed to two or three horizontal, triangular-section arris rails fixed between concrete or timber posts in slots. Boards are feathered-edged (thinner at one edge than the other) and measure about 100mm (4in) or 150mm (6in) wide; the wide edge of one overlaps the narrow edge of its neighbour. Gravel boards, which run between the posts at ground level, protect the bases of the boards from attack by rot, and can be renewed.

These fences are normally assembled on site from separate components. Versions with feather-edged boards nailed horizontally to the posts are also made.

Interwoven panels are one of the cheapest types of solid fences. Panels are made from thin larch or pine slats between 75mm (3in) and 100mm (4in) wide, which are interwoven horizontally around vertical battens to form a basketweave. This is framed with battens and the panels nailed through the frame to the posts. They're sold in 1.8m (6ft) widths, with heights between 600mm (2ft) and 1.8m (6ft).

Wavey-edged panels are made by fixing thin, irregular-edged larch or pine planks within a softwood frame. Planks overlap as in a closeboard arrangement. Panel sizes are the same as interwoven types.

Picket fencing is a boundary typically used in front gardens, and rarely exceeding 1.2 m (4ft) high. Vertical 'pales' – commonly painted, often pointed or decoratively shaped at the top – are nailed to arris rails at about 50mm (2in) intervals; the rails are fixed between posts spaced about 2m (6ft 6in) to 3m (10ft) apart. Palisade fencing is a version with pales butted together.

Post-and-rail fencing consists of posts with horizontal rails nailed or notched into them. Posts are either round and rails round or half-round, or square in section. Ranch-style fencing is similar, with thinner, planed rails for painting nailed to short posts.

Rustic fences made of wooden poles complete with bark, give a natural-looking lightweight barrier or frame for climbers.

Repairing fences

Any part of a fence that comes into contact with the damp ground is susceptible to deterioration. If a post has started to rot at the

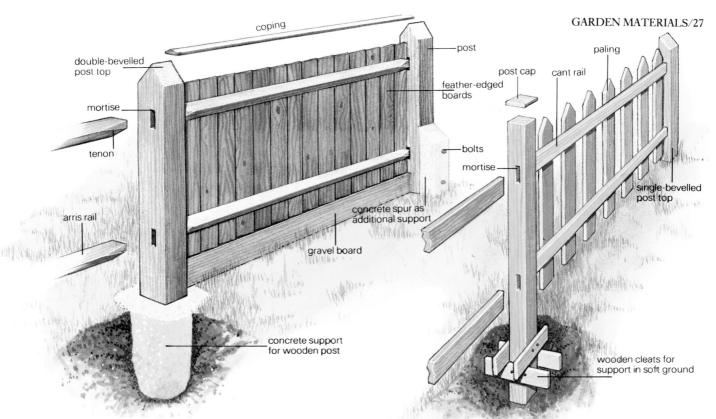

coping

post

double-bevelled post top

feather-edged boards

mortise

tenon

bolts

arris rail

concrete spur as additional support

gravel board

concrete support for wooden post

post cap

cant rail

paling

mortise

single-bevelled post top

wooden cleats for support in soft ground

base, you don't need to replace it entirely: remove the rotten section and secure the post with a pre-cast concrete spur.

Dig a hole about 600mm (2ft) deep next to the rotten post and fill the base with hardcore. Ram this down with a sledge hammer or stout post. Lower the spur in the hole, bevelled top outermost. Set it vertically, using a spirit level.

Mark the fence post through the pre-drilled holes in the spur, lift out the spur and drill holes for the coach bolts supplied for fixing. Replace the spur and hammer the coach bolts through the post into the spur from the other side of the fence. Slip on washers and secure and tighten the bolts with nuts.

Ram more hardcore around the spur then fill the hole with a coarse concrete mix.

Metal fence spikes are available for securing a rickety fence post (it's a good way to fit new posts, too). The spike, which is driven into the ground below the post, has a socket at the top into which the fence post is slotted and retained with galvanized nails in some models.

A badly rotten post should be replaced with a new one, and it's usually possible to do this without having to dismantle the entire fence. On a closeboard fence, prise off about three boards from each side of the post using a claw hammer. If it is not possible to remove the post without cutting the arris rails where they're located in the sockets; first prop the fence on both sides with wooden struts nailed to the top arris. Saw through the arris rails flush with the

sides of the post, using a panel saw. The post will probably be set in a concrete block below ground. Dig around the base to expose the concrete. The post and fixing is likely to be very heavy, so you'll need to rig up a lever to extract it from the hole.

Drive two 100mm (4in) long nails about half-way into each side of the post, about 300mm (1ft) from the base. Bind strong rope or nylon twine around the post directly below the nails. Leave a long length of rope extra. Pile a stack of bricks about 600mm (2ft) away from the post so they're about 100mm (4in) higher than the level of the nails.

Lay a length of stout timber on the bricks and butt one end up to the original post. Drive two more nails half-way into each side about 110mm (4in) from the end. Bind the loose end of rope around the lever arm, wrapping it around the nails.

To raise the post (get a helper to support it first) lean your weight firmly down on the other end of the horizontal post to lever it out of the hole.

Fill the base of the hole with about 150mm (6in) of hardcore to give a firm, free-draining base and ram this down well with a sledge hammer or stout post. Lower the new post into the hole and set it vertically. Support it with two wooden battens temporarily nailed near the top and placed at right-angles to each other.

Add more broken bricks or concrete around the post and ram it well down. Mix up some coarse concrete and tip it into the hole. Pack the mix around the post to dispel

Above *Two popular types of fence. Closeboard fences (left) are solid, durable and the ideal garden boundaries: posts are set in the ground in concrete sleeves, connected by horizontal arris rails and clad with vertical feather-edged boards, which overlap each other. Picket fences (right) are typically used in front gardens. Horizontal cant rails are mortised into posts and are clad with vertical palings, commonly pointed or rounded at the top, usually spaced apart.*

1. *To replace a rotten closeboarded fence post, lever off the boards.*
2. *Dig out the earth around the fence post, as far down as the concrete sleeving.*
3. *Drive a nail in each side of the post and wrap strong rope around it. Pile up a stack of bricks.*
4. *Construct a lever using a stout post. Drive in nails, wrap the rope around and pull down to lift the post from its hole.*
5. *Dig out the hole, line with hardcore, then insert the new post.*
6. *Shovel in a coarse concrete mix to secure the post upright.*
7. *Refix the sawn ends of the arris rails to the new post be screwing on a galvanised metal repair bracket.*
8. *Slide the boards back under their neighbours, set vertically then secure with galvanized nails.*

air pockets, then shape the top into a bevel. Allow the concrete to harden overnight before refixing the fencing.

Refix the arris rails to the post using galvanized metal arris rail brackets: a long, angled arm fits along the rail and splayed ends fit against the post. Secure with 50mm (2in) long galvanized clout nails. (You can fix an arris rail that's snapped midway with an angled repair bracket without splayed ends; it's simply nailed across the fracture.)

Nail the feather-edged boards back on each side of the post.

Gravel boards that are rotten can be replaced. Lever off the board with a claw hammer; it will be nailed to small blocks of 38 × 25mm (1½ × 1in) softwood called 'cleats' and these may need to be replaced, too. Measure between the posts and cut a new length of 150 × 25mm (6 × 1in) softwood for the new gravel board, plus two new cleats. Treat the wood thoroughly with a good preservative treatment.

Fix the new cleats to the sides of the fence posts with 38mm (1½in) galvanized nails, set back 25mm (1in) from the face. Position the gravel board on the cleats, butted up to the bottoms of the feather-edged boards and secure with nails.

Feather-edged boards are very thin and consequently easily damaged. To replace a defective board within a section, extract its nails with a pair of pincers, then wiggle it free. If you can't grasp the nail heads with the pincers, punch them all the way through the board using a centre punch or a large blunt nail and hammer.

Cut a new board, treat it with preservative, then slot its thin edge under the thick edge of the adjacent board. Secure to the arris rail with a galvanized nail driven through its face.

You can refix a whole row of boards in the same way, but be sure to check the vertical alignment about every third board, using a spirit level.

1. *Gravel boards are usually the first to rot. Lever them off, plus their cleats, then nail on new cleats.*
2. *Nail a new length of gravel board to the cleats: the boards should be flush with the fence post and butted up to the bottoms of the boards.*

Strong winds can catch a flimsy panel fence and blow it down. Although it's easy to refix the panel; by nailing through its frame into the post as before, the frame is made of quite thin wood and it may have split. A firmer fixing is to use galvanized metal brackets.

Nail two of the U-shaped brackets to the posts about 150mm (6in) from top and bottom, using 50mm (2in) nails. Slot the panel into the channels and retain by nailing through the side flaps into the frame.

You can easily cut a panel fence to size to fit a space. Hold the panel against the gap and mark off the overlap. Scribe down the panel at this point. Prise off the end battens from both sides and refix them inside your marked line. The end battens usually extend up to the top of the top rail, but set them beneath it in the new position, leaving the excess protruding at the base of the panel. Saw off the ends of the battens then carefully saw down the surplus slats against the edge of the battens. Fit the panel in place and secure to the post.

The open-grained tops of fence posts are prone to penetration by rainwater, so it's wise to finish them off to ensure water doesn't linger. Cut the top to a steep chamfer, or a double-bevel and apply preservative liberally. Alternatively, nail on a pre-made hardwood cap, which has four bevels. Additionally, or instead, cover the top of the post with nailed sheet metal.

To discourage rot at ground level, drill a downward-sloping hole near the base and pour in preservative. Then plug the hole.

Bricks, blocks and stone

Bricks, blocks and stone can be used to create numerous structures in the garden, from practical boundary walls, planters and barbecues to decorative arches and functional flights of steps.

Choosing bricks

Bricks are made from fire-burnt clay (a process that gives them their strength and durability), concrete, or calcium silicate (sand limes). Clay bricks are graded for quality: ask for 'special quality' if you're building in exposed conditions or 'ordinary' for general use. Calcium silicate bricks come in six grades: from class two, the weakest, to class seven, the strongest.

To add to the confusion, bricks are also given names that reflect their colour, texture, and place of origin. Stocks and Flettons are common examples, but choice doesn't influence usage.

Bricks are made in a standard metric size – 225 × 112.5 × 75mm, which conforms roughly to the old Imperial size of $8^7/_8$ × $4^3/_8$ × 3in: an important point when you're matching new brickwork to old. These are 'nominal' dimensions: the actual size is 10mm ($^3/_8$in) less all round to allow for a normal mortar joint.

Of the hundreds of brick types available, there are basically three types you're likely to use in garden construction:

Facing bricks are intended to be used where an attractive appearance is needed and come in various colours and either rough or smooth textures. 'Faced' bricks have only one or two attractive sides, whereas facing bricks are good-looking all round.

Common bricks are usually used where an attractive appearance isn't necessary. They're cheaper than other bricks.

Engineering bricks are hard, dense and impervious to water. They're usually used

1. Facing bricks, made from clay or calcium silicate, are used where an attractive appearance is wanted. They can be rough or smooth, hard or soft, and come in a range of attractive colours.
2. Common bricks are fairly rough in appearance and used for their practical qualities or where they're to be rendered.
3. Engineering bricks are the hardest and most durable bricks, ideal for use where they're likely to come into contact with damp.

1

2

3

in damp conditions and are quite expensive. Two classes (A or B) are made, referring to strength and water resistance.

Numerous special-shaped bricks are made to give a decorative or protective finish to structures. Typical types include rounded-end 'bullheads' for completing a wall; half-round copings to neaten the top of a wall; radial stretchers for curved walls.

Some bricks have an indent in one face, called the 'frog', which forms a good bond with the mortar. The frog is normally laid uppermost. Other bricks have holes pierced through them, which serve the same purpose.

Setting out

When you're building a wall, it's vital that it runs in a straight line and is level through-out, so set up stringlines to act as a guide. For greatest accuracy, set up 'profile boards' (use the boards to mark out footings, too). Drive two 25mm sq (1in sq) wooden pegs into the ground at each end of the proposed wall, spaced slightly wider apart than the wall. Nail a length of 50 × 25mm (2 × 1in) softwood across the tops of the pegs.

Fix nails in the tops of the cross pieces to mark the outer edges of the wall and string lines between them.

Bricks are laid in an overlapping 'bond' to create a rigid structure and to spread the load. Single thickness (half-brick) walls are always laid in a 'running' bond; bricks are laid end to end with their long, stretcher, faces showing. Alternate rows are staggered by half a brick's length so that no

vertical joints are seen to align.

Double-thickness (single-brick) walls include courses of 'headers' – bricks laid across the width of the wall with their end faces visible.

Laying bricks

Before you start to lay bricks, check the layout of the bond by placing the first few courses dry, without mortar. Place each brick a finger-width apart to allow for the joints.

Mix up sufficient cement and soft sand mortar and trowel a very thin screed down the length of the foundation slab, between the stringlines. Use a spirit level held vertically against the stringline to transfer their positions down to the screed. Mark the mortar with your trowel at each end of the foundations and scribe along against a straight-edge.

Trowel a 10mm (³/₈in) thick screed in between the scored lines. Run your trowel back over the mortar to form ridges, which aid the adhesion of the mortar through suction. Place your first brick into position on the screed (frog uppermost). Press the brick down gently with a sideways motion to bed it evenly. Tap it carefully with the handle of your trowel then scoop off any surplus mortar that's squeezed out underneath (you can use this to form the next joint).

Butter one end of another brick with mortar to form a vertical joint: scrape the mortar off the trowel onto the brick. Form it into a wedge. Place the brick on the screed,

1. *Trowel a thin screed of mortar underneath your guide strings and score a line along it, using a spirit level as a guide, to indicate the first course of bricks.*
2. *Lay the first brick on a bed of mortar then butter the end of the second brick, forming a wedge-shape for a good joint.*
3. *Place the second brick against the first, aligned with the string. Level it by tapping with your trowel handle then scoop off excess mortar.*
4. *As the courses progress, use stringlines and pins to ensure the brickwork is rising evenly. Move up the strings with each course.*

butting up the mortared end to the first brick. Tap the brick into place gently and scoop away any surplus mortar. Continue to lay bricks in this way until you complete the first course.

Check that the bricks are level across the top using a long spirit level. Adjust the thickness of the mortar bed if necessary. Check also that the row is straight, by holding your spirit level or a long straight-edge against the side.

To lay the second and subsequent course, trowel mortar onto the preceding course and bed the bricks on top. Remember, no vertical joint must align: in a stretcher-bond wall you'll have to start and finish the alternate rows with a cut brick. If you're building a corner, however, set the brick at right-angles to the other to start the new leaf.

It's usual to build up the corners or'ends of a wall first, forming a stepped structure; this 'racking back' ensures that the wall rises squarely. Fill in between the corners or racked ends in the normal way. Stretch a stringline between the ends as a guide to laying the intermediate bricks. Insert a nail in the mortar joint at each end to hold the string taut (or use special bricklayer's pins) and move the string up for subsequent courses.

Check that the courses are rising with consistently thick joints using a 'gauge rod'. Make this from a 1m (3ft 3in) length of 50 × 25mm (2 × 1in) softwood marked off in 75mm (3in) increments (brick height plus a 10mm (³/₈in) mortar joint). To use the rod,

hold it against the end of the wall: the marks should align with the top of each brick if the courses are correct. Also check that the wall isn't bowing out by holding a spirit level or straightedge diagonally across the face.

You'll need to cut some bricks to size to achieve a proper bonding arrangement. Mark off the amount to be cut by scoring around the brick against another brick. Place the brick on grass or a layer of sand and tap gently around it, along the scored line, using a club hammer and bolster chisel. To break the brick cleanly, lay it frog down and tap sharply on the scored line with the chisel.

Replacing a damaged brick

Constantly exposed to the elements, it's hardly surprising that masonry can deteriorate. Common problems are crumbly mortar joints that loosen the bricks and make the structure dangerous, and cracks running through the bricks or joints.

It's possible to replace a single damaged brick (or a small area) within an area of masonry without damaging the surrounding bricks. (Don't attempt to replace more than about ten bricks without propping up the rest of the masonry.)

Drill a row of closely-spaced holes in the mortar joints surrounding the damaged brick, using a 10mm (³/₈in) diameter masonry bit in an electric drill. Hack out the weakened mortar using a slim, cold chisel or a special 'plugging chisel' and a club hammer. Lever out the brick with a bolster chisel, but if it's stubborn, break it up by

1. *To replace a damaged brick, drill through the mortar joints around the brick, using a 10mm (³/₈in) masonry bit.*
2. *Chop out the weakened mortar using a plugging chisel and club hammer.*
3. *Lever out the brick using a bolster chisel, breaking it into pieces if necessary.*
4. *Clean up the loose dust and debris from the hole, then dampen the masonry with clean water.*
5. *Spread a layer of mortar onto the base of the hole and one end, and furrow the surface with the trowel.*
6. *Butter the top and one end of the replacement brick with mortar and furrow it to improve the suction.*
7. *Insert the new brick into the hole and tap it into position with the handle of the trowel.*
8. *Neaten up the mortar pointing between the replacement brick and the others, following the joint profile.*

To repair spalled brickwork:
1. *Mix mortar with brick dust, apply PVA adhesive to the spalled brick, then spread on the mortar, using a batten to protect the pointing.*
2. *The repaired brick will look darker than the surrounding masonry, but will lighten as the mortar dries.*

To repair defective pointing:
1. *Rake out the loose, crumbly pointing with a plugging chisel.*
2. *Finish off the joints with new mortar, following the original pointing profile.*

drilling into it many times. If you're removing more bricks, you can easily chop into the mortar joints to release them.

Clean up all around the hole then brush out dust and debris. Dampen inside the hole with water so the bricks won't suck the water out of the repair mortar too quickly and cause it to crack. Mix up some bricklaying mortar from a small dry-mixed bag then trowel a 10mm (³/₈in) thick bed onto the base of the hole. Scrape some mortar up one side of the hole.

Butter the top and one end of the replacement brick (try to obtain a matching replacement: demolition sites and builders' yards are good sources) and insert it in the hole, buttered end to non-mortared end of the hole. Tap the brick gently into place with the handle of your trowel so it's flush with the surrounding masonry. Repeat the procedure for other bricks. Finally, point the joint around the brick with more mortar, matching the profile to that of the surrounding wall.

Curing spalled brickwork
Old bricks are prone to a condition called 'spalling': water penetrates the faces, freezes and breaks off the outer surface. Spalled brickwork not only looks ugly but also, if left unattended, the bricks will disintegrate.

Where a brick is badly spalled, replace it; if it's only slightly damaged, a simple, effective repair can be made. Mix up some mortar with a proprietary cement colourant powder, added according to the manufacturer's instructions. If you can't obtain a suitable match, substitute brick dust for the colourant.

Brush any loose material from the spalled brick then paint on a strong solution of PVA adhesive and water. Hold a length of thin wood over the mortar joint below the spalled brick to protect it from smears, then trowel the mortar mix over the primed surface. Carefully shape the mortar to resemble the profiles of the other bricks and leave to set. The repair will appear dark at first, but will dry lighter.

Pointing brickwork
The mortar joints are usually shaped into one of four 'pointing profiles', which deflect rainwater and prevent it from soaking between the bricks. To prepare a wall for repointing, rake out the joints to about 10mm (³/₈in) with a plugging chisel and brush out dust and debris. Wet the joints and refill with new mortar (pointing mortar is sold in bags dry-mixed, to which you add water). Apply the profiles with a small pointing trowel while the mortar is still wet.

● **Weathered** Starting with the horizontals, press the blade of the trowel onto the mortar and angle it inwards at the top. Slide the trowel downwards off the brick below to form a neat V-shape. Angle the vertical either way.
● **Flush** Rub a wad of sacking or hessian over the mortar when it has started to dry.
● **Rounded** Rub a length of 10mm (³/8in) diameter tube or dowelling along the joints for a curved effect.
● **Raked** Rub the joint with a thin piece of rectangular section wood to give a recessed profile. Only suitable for sheltered sites.

Concrete walling blocks

Bricks can sometimes look too formal, especially in a 'cottagey' garden, but decorative walling blocks, which have the appearance of natural stone, offer a real alternative. They're moulded into handy units that can be laid just like bricks.

Blocks are available in various sizes, with a choice of split or pitched faces (not all faces are textured; only one long face and one end should be exposed). The blocks are concrete but some have natural stone aggregates added in manufacture to give an authentic look; numerous colours are available, such as greens, yellows, reds, greys and buff tones.

Modular blocks moulded to look like several smaller coursed stones can be used to save time in building. Treat them just like single blocks and lay them with mortar. For a double-sided wall, however, you'll need to lay two skins of blocks, as there's only one textured side.

Large-format rectangular blocks intended as single-skin, double-sided walling come with both sides textured. Matching pilasters with hollow centres to take reinforcing rods are made with some blocks to build supporting piers. Coping and cappings for the wall can be stuck on with mortar.

For a more formal but still decorative wall offering partial screening while still permitting breezes to flow through, choose screen walling blocks. Moulded from concrete with various pierced geometric patterns, they're laid in 'stack bond', one on top of the other, instead of being overlapped. Consequently, they're not structurally strong. The blocks, which usually measure 300 × 300 × 100mm (12 × 12 × 4in), slot into channelled, hollow pilasters, which are stacked to make piers. Capping and copings complete the wall.

Drystone walling gives an attractive, 'country' air to a garden, but suitable stones are not easy – or cheap – to obtain, and the construction requires quite some skill to perfect. You may, however, be able to make low walls using stones bought from a garden centre or quarry. For a similar effect, try manufactured drystone walling blocks, which are laid in the same way without mortar.

If your requirements for a building material are purely functional, use large-format concrete blocks (breeze blocks). These moulded units measure 150–225mm (6–9in) high × 450mm (18in), 600mm (24in), and 620mm (24½in) long and 50–300mm (2–12in) thick. Various densities are made for a range of uses.

Building a rockery

Natural stone is ideal for making a rock garden. You can buy suitable rocks from a garden centre or quarry, and some hollow manufactured rocks are also made.

A rockery demands good drainage and you may have to build a soakaway beneath it (see page 11).

You'll need about 1,500kg (25cwt) of stone to build a rockery about 3m (10ft) wide and 400mm (16in) high above ground level.

Mark out the site with strings and pegs then dig out the topsoil to a depth of 150mm (6in) and retain it. Compact the soil in the hole then prepare a free-draining bedding material: mix one part grit to five parts topsoil or compost then refill the hole to a depth of 50mm (2in) below ground level.

Move the largest 'key' stone into place at the base of the rockery and pack soil under it. Add medium-sized stones, forming an L-shaped outcrop; stones should become smaller towards the back. Lean each stone back into the bank by about 15 degrees.

Fill inside the outcrop with the soil/grit mixture to just over the tops of the stones, then add a second L-shaped outcrop behind the first. Repeat the process until

Below Reconstituted stone walling blocks come in various sizes and colours; copings are wider and pier cappings are square.

Bottom Used like bricks, blocks can be built up course by course to create a natural-looking wall with a rough-textured face.

1. *When mixing concrete by hand, pour the cement right into the centre of the aggregate.*
2. *Mix the two substances together thoroughly until they are the same colour and consistency.*
3. *Form a crater in the middle of the cement mix and slowly add water. Mix well until the right consistency.*

you reach the pinnacle, which should be topped with small stones. Cover all exposed soil with a layer of grit then plant out the terraces with suitable alpine plants and dwarf shrubs and bulbs.

Concrete in the garden

Cast concrete is an extremely versatile and economical material, used typically for foundations for a garden wall, a base for a shed or coal bunker – or in its own right as a surface for a path or patio.

Concrete is a mix of Portland cement, combined aggregate, sometimes called ballast (sharp sand and stones), and water. The cement and water form a paste that bonds the particles together into a dense, strong material that can be moulded.

Garden structures such as walls must be set on a firm base to spread their load and prevent sinking. The most basic foundation is a strip of concrete, called 'footings', cast in a trench.

Larger 'rafts' are used to make bases for garden buildings and as paths and driveways. They're cast in a timber frame, called 'formwork', then compacted and levelled.

Buying concrete

There are various ways to buy concrete, largely dependent on the amount you need. For very small jobs and repairs, for example, just buy pre-packed dry-mixes with the ingredients properly proportioned for you. Dry-mix is sold in DIY stores in bags from 2.5kg (5½lb) to 50kg (1cwt). All you do is add the water.

Some minor repairs to concrete can be made using mortar, which is concrete but without the large particles of aggregate (see below).

For larger jobs, it is more economical to

buy the ingredients separately in bulk from a builders' merchant and mix them yourself by hand or hired mixing machine (see pages 69–71). For extensive jobs requiring over 3 cu m (4 cu yd) of concrete (making a drive, for example), buy ready-mixed. It's delivered by mixer lorry and can be deposited directly into your prepared base, so long as there's access for the vehicle. You can't dawdle over this job: be prepared to cast, compact and level the mix in just a few hours (less on a hot day) or it will harden.

Various strengths of concrete are required for certain jobs and this is determined by the ratio of ingredients (by volume) used in the mix. Most concrete work in the garden will call for one of three basic mixes, as shown in the chart below, along with its relevant usage.

If a mix is described as 1:2:3 (a general purpose mix), as in the first example, this means one volume of cement; two volumes of sand; three volumes of aggregate.

Builders' merchants often sell the sharp sand and gravel aggregate already combined as 'all-in ballast'. The size of the aggregate is important for the texture of the mix, and ranges in size from about 10mm (⅜in) to 20mm (¾in) for fine and coarse mixes respectively. The same general purpose mix, therefore, translates as 20mm 1:4 ballast; this means that there are no particles in the mix larger than 20mm (¾in) and that you'll need one part cement to four parts all-in ballast per batch. Use a bucket to proportion mixes.

How much concrete

Calculating the amount of concrete you'll need for a particular job is quite straightforward. First work out the volume of your project in cubic metres (cubic yards) by multiplying length × width × thickness in

CONCRETE MIXES	Mix-your own			Ready-mix
Use	Proportions (volume)	Amount per cu m (cu yd)	Yield per 50kg/ 1cwt bag cement	specification
General purpose (Most uses except foundations and exposed paving)	Cement 1 Sand 2 20mm (¾in) aggr. 3 or all-in ballast 4	6.4 bags 680kg (13cwt) 1175kg (23½cwt) 1855kg (36cwt)	0.15 cu m (5 cu ft)	C20P to BS 5328, medium to high workability, 20mm (¾in) max. aggregate size
Foundation (Footings, foundations and bases for precast paving)	Cement 1 Sand 2½ 20mm (¾in) aggr. 3½ or all-in ballast 5	5.6 bags 720kg (14cwt) 1165kg (23cwt) 1885kg (37cwt)	0.18 cu m (6 cu ft)	C7.5P to BS 5328, high workability, 20mm (¾in) max aggregate size
Paving (All exposed in situ paving, especially drives)	Cement 1 Sand 1½ 20mm (¾in) aggr. 2½ or all-in ballast 3½	8 bags 600kg (11cwt) 1200kg (23½cwt) 1800kg (35½cwt)	0.12 cu m (4 cu ft)	Special prescribed mix minimum cement content 33kg/m³; 4% entrained air; target slump 75mm (3in)

metres (yards). Add 10 per cent for wastage.

Study the fourth column in the chart, which gives the yield of mixed concrete per 50kg (1cwt) bag of cement, to determine the quantities of ingredients you'll need.

Ordering the correct amount and proportions of ready-mix is much simpler: you leave it up the supplier. He'll need to know the volume you require, its purpose (so he can work out a suitable mix), the delivery date, site access details, and how you propose to handle it on delivery.

The chart shows the specification for each mix, consisting of the mix number, the Standard, followed by the consistency and aggregate size.

If you're mixing your own concrete from bulk ingredients, proper storage of materials is important. Cement must be protected from moisture or it will harden: keep it in a garage or shed if posisible, or raised above the ground by about 100mm (4in) on a platform. If the bags are stored outside, cover the pile with polythene sheeting weighted down.

Mixing by hand

To mix concrete by hand, shovel the cement onto the aggregate and gradually mix the two until they're uniform in colour by heaping them into a 'volcano'.

Form a crater in the heap and add some water. Collapse the walls of the volcano and mix in the ingredients. Add more water a little at a time and mix to achieve a uniform colour and consistency. Beware of adding too much water, or you'll ruin the mix.

Turn the mix into a new pile three times to make sure the ingredients are thoroughly combined. Draw your shovel back across the heap in steps: the ridges should be firm and slump-free, without a residue of runny cement.

Mixing by machine

Small machine mixers are available for hire and take much of the toil out of mixing your own concrete. Add half the coarse aggregate and half the water to the mixer drum, then the sand. Start the motor and let the ingredients mix for a few minutes, then add all the cement and what's left of the coarse aggregate and the water. Mix until the concrete is of a consistency that it falls off the blades cleanly. Tip the mixer drum to empty the contents into a waiting barrow. Add the aggregate and water for the next batch while you're placing the first batch and leave the drum revolving to keep the blades clean.

Laying footings

Footings for a garden wall or other small brick or block structure must measure twice the width of the masonry and half as deep, and there must be a projection at each end that's half the width of the masonry. This spreads the load of the wall to firm ground. If your wall is 225mm (9in) wide (a single brick length) the margins around it will need to be about 112mm (4¾in). Deeper footings will be necessary if the structure rises above about seven courses of bricks.

To set out the footings, stretch strings between wooden stakes driven into the ground at each end of the proposed foundations; space them apart the width of the trench. If the foundation is to be built flush against a concrete path or drive, you'll only need a single stringline.

Hold a spirit level vertically against the stringlines and mark the ground directly below each line; connect the lines by scribing against a long timber straightedge with a trowel. Alternatively, sprinkle a line of sand under the strings.

Remove the strings, but not the stakes, and dig down to the correct depth. Keep the trench sides vertical and the floor flat.

You can cast the concrete directly on a well-compacted earth base, but where the soil is soft, add a layer of hardcore (broken bricks and concrete) and ram it down well using a sledge hammer or alternatively a stout timber post.

Below: *Mix mortar by hand for small quantities. Use a spotboard to contain the mix close the job.*
1. Use strings stretched between wooden stakes fitted with cross pieces to mark the width of strip foundations.
2. Dig the trench and set timber pegs vertically in the base, level them with a spirit level and use to set the concrete to the correct depth.

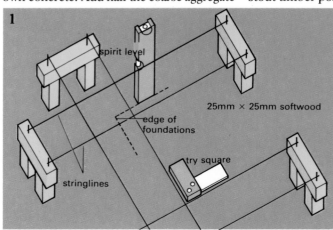

1

spirit level

edge of foundations

25mm × 25mm softwood

try square

stringlines

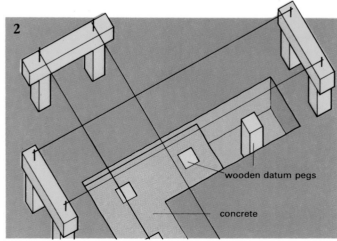

2

wooden datum pegs

concrete

The concrete strip must be truly flat and horizontal, so timber datum pegs are used to indicate the final level. Cut enough 25mm square (1in sq) softwood pegs to be spaced at 1m (3ft) intervals along the trench; drive in the first peg so it protrudes by the depth of the concrete. Hammer in the remaining pegs. Level them with the first peg by spanning across their tops with a spirit level on a straightedge.

Mix up sufficient concrete to fill the trench, tip it in and work it around with a shovel to expel air bubbles. Add more concrete until it's just above the level of the pegs. Roughly level the surface with the back of your shovel then check with a straightedge between the peg tops to highlight voids or highspots. Add or remove concrete accordingly.

Use a length of stout timber to compact the mix and flatten the surface, in a chopping motion, moving across the strip about 50mm (2in) at a time. Leave overnight (preferably longer) to dry before starting to build on the footings.

During hot weather, cover the concrete with old sacking, kept moist to prevent too-rapid drying out of the mix, which could cause cracks. You shouldn't lay concrete during very cold weather but if a snap frost occurs, cover the slab with polythene sheeting over a layer of straw or blanket loft insulation to protect it.

Casting a large slab

A large concrete slab for a path or patio, or as a base for a a garden building, must be cast within timber formwork set at the perimeter of the site. Slab thickness depends on what the base is to be used for, but about 100–125mm (4–5in) over 75mm (3in) of hardcore is adequate for a drive; 75–100mm (3–4in) for a shed base.

Mark out the shape of your slab with strings and pegs, making sure you get the corners exactly at 90 degrees. Make a 'builder's square' from three lengths of 50 × 25mm (2 × 1in) softwood cut in the proportions 3:4:5 – 300mm; 400mm; 500mm/(12in; 16in; 20in). Nail them together with a half-lap at the right-angled

corner and with the longest side nailed on top of the other two sides. Use a straight-edge tool to check the angles.

Dig out the topsoil to the depth of the slab. Allow an extra margin all round for access. As with footings, the slab must be level over its whole area. To ensure this, drive 300mm (1ft) long 25mm square (1in sq) softwood pegs into the base at 1.5m (5ft) intervals, so the tops are level with the finished height of the concrete. Align the pegs with a spirit level on a long straight-edge, as described in Chapter One, page 7–8.

Excavate the base accordingly. Add well-rammed hardcore to firm up soft ground. On long paths and drives you can level the base using sighting rods.

To make the formwork you'll need some planks of sawn softwood 25mm (1in) thick and as wide as the depth of the concrete, and some 50mm square (2in sq) softwood pegs about 300mm (1ft) long. Drive the pegs into the ground, outside the slab area, at about 1m (3ft 4in) intervals. Set the planks level and secure them to the pegs with nails.

A large slab or long path must slope to one side slightly to ensure rapid drainage of rainwater, and this must be incorporated in the setting out. Place a small offcut of timber (called a 'shim') under your spirit level when levelling the pegs and form-boards, at what will be the lower end. When the spirit level registers horizontal, the fall is correct.

Tip barrowloads of concrete into the base then compact the mix and level it with the top of the formwork. On a wide slab, you'll need assistance: use a stout tamping beam in a chopping action. Allow the concrete to harden before prising off the formwork then fill the margin around the perimeter with earth. Don't put the slab to use for about ten days.

Repairing cracks

A cracked, chipped or crumbly concrete surface looks unsightly, and paves the way for more widespread deterioration. Cracks usually appear after a hard winter, when frost penetrates crevices and expands.

To repair cracked or chipped concrete slab:
1. *Enlarge the crack to about 12–20mm (½–¾) wide using a club hammer and cold chisel, undercutting the edges to improve the grip of the filler.*
2. *Brush out dust and debris then daub on some PVA adhesive, which aids the adhesion of the mortar.*
3. *Spread some mortar into the crack, chopping with the trowel blade to force it into every crevice. Smooth it level.*
4. *Ram broken bricks into a hole in concrete using the handle of a club hammer, then apply mortar.*

1

2

3
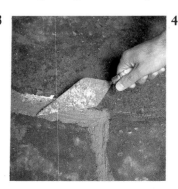

4

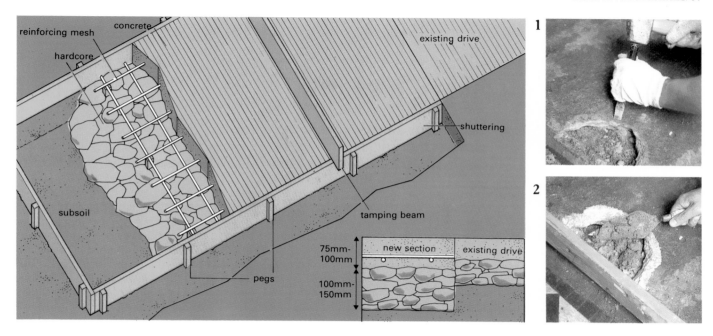

labels: reinforcing mesh, concrete, hardcore, existing drive, shuttering, subsoil, tamping beam, pegs, 75mm–100mm, 100mm–150mm, new section, existing drive

Check for signs of subsidence; if the trouble is localized, simply patch the damage. If it's more extensive, renew the section.

Enlarge the crack to about 12–20mm (½–¾in) wide, using a club hammer and cold chisel. Under-cut the edges to provide a grip for the repair material. Brush out dust and debris with a stiff-bristled brush. To aid the adhesion of the patch, apply a liberal coat of PVA adhesive mixed with water (in the proportion 1:5) to the crack and allow to dry. Paint on a second coat of a stronger solution (3 parts PVA to one of water) then apply mortar while it's tacky.

Mix up some repair mortar in a bucket in a ratio of 1:3 cement/soft sand. Trowel the mortar into the crack, pressing it right into the sides. Force it into place by chopping with the trowel blade. Smooth the patch off level with the surrounding surface.

Filling holes

Holes are often caused by localised subsidence in the hardcore foundations. To repair this defect, widen the hole just enough to undercut the edges.

Ram some broken bricks deep into the hole using a stout length of wood or the shaft of your club hammer. Make up a concrete mix of 1:5 all-in ballast (see page 34), prime the hole with a PVA adhesive solution, then trowel in the mix, overfilling slightly. Compact the mix using a length of timber to give a fairly rough finish.

Renewing a section of concrete

A section of a drive or path that's seriously cracked or subsided due to a fault in the sub-base should be broken up and relaid anew. Hire a heavy-duty jack hammer (see

pages 69–71) and break up the affected area. Cut neatly across the sound section.

You can use the old broken-up concrete and hardcore as your sub-base, so long as it's well-rammed down. Set datum pegs in the soil to set the level of the concrete flush with the adjoining sound surface. If the ground below the subsided area is light, sandy soil, include a reinforcing mesh in the new slab. This is available in rolls from builders' merchants: you'll need 100mm square (4in sq) steel mesh made with 6mm (¼in) diameter wire.

Dig the foundations deeper than before and allow for a thicker slab. Hire a motorized plate compactor (see pages 69–71) to firm the hardcore, or use a garden roller. Rig up timber formwork nailed to pegs at the perimeter of the site and lay the mesh over the hardcore.

Mix up the concrete and pour into the formwork box. Compact the mix, making sure it's well butted up to the hard concrete edge, then tamp it level with the formboards.

Repairing crumbly edges

The edges of concrete slabs are their weakest, most vulnerable parts. Chop back the crumbly material to a sound edge and prime the edge with two coats of PVA solution. Fix a length of timber about 25mm (1in) thick and the depth of the concrete, across the front of the broken edge to mould the repair concrete. Secure it with wooden pegs driven into the ground.

Mix up some concrete and trowel it into the hole. Use a chopping action with the blade of your trowel to work the mix under the edge of the hard concrete, then compact it. Remove the formboard when the concrete has hardened fully.

Above left *If you need to renew a section of concrete, dig up the old part and lay new, deeper hardcore foundations. Set reinforcing mesh in the layer of new concrete to prevent the trouble occurring again. Undercut the edge of the old concrete to give a good key for the new concrete.*

1. *To repair a crumbly edge, chop back the material to sound concrete using a cold chisel.*
2. *Place a timber batten across the edge of the concrete, then trowel in fresh mortar. Leave to set before removing the batten.*

CHAPTER 3

RUNNING THE GARDEN

Make your garden an efficient, orderly place to work by installing electric lighting, power and water on tap. You'll discover just how easy and convenient it is to tend your plants – and you'll be able to make full use of the plot, even at night.

No garden will look after itself. Left unattended, the plot will soon deteriorate into an overgrown jungle that's unkempt, unhealthy, and unworkable.

Regular grass mowing, weeding and watering are only half the battle. Plants need special care if they're to thrive and treatments with fertilizers will certainly give them the boost they may need.

The garden itself should be run with precision to keep it free from blight and the debris that has a habit of expanding – old prunings, hedge trimmings, weeds and other unwanted matter. What's useful can be committed to the compost heap; what's useless can be burned.

To speed the efficient gardener about his work (leaving time for relaxing with the fruits of his labours) the garden should be equipped with the necessary supplies: power for today's electrical gadgets (and light for the patio); water on tap for greenhouse and fish pond.

An outside tap

An outside tap offers a host of benefits. A tap fitted to your house wall, at the end of the plot (or even in both locations) makes chores such as sprinkling the lawn and watering plants so much easier and less disruptive. You can banish the trailing hose from the house, and free the kitchen tap. Additionally, you'll find an outside tap a real saviour when you're involved in messy building work such as mixing concrete, or car-washing.

Installing an outside tap into your mains water supply is a straightforward plumbing project that's made even simpler by the many DIY kits on the market.

Before you go any further, consult your local water authority: you may be limited in your choice of tap components by local restrictions – in some areas any work carried out on the rising main must be done by an authorised plumber. You will have to pay more water rates for an extra tap.

Whatever components you choose, the installation is virtually the same: the new tap and its pipework are simply connected into the house's rising main.

Choosing components

If you opt for individual components rather than a kit, you'll need a purpose-made garden bib tap (sold by garden centres and builders' or plumbers' merchants) in rustless brass. It has an inclined crutch-type handle for easy use and usually comes with a wall bracket.

You'll also need a stopvalve to isolate the supply pipe so it can be drained in winter in case of frost.

To complete the system you'll need sufficient 15mm diameter copper pipe to reach the break-in point, plus various elbow fittings (compression or capillary) and a tee fitting to connect into the mains. (If you have an old-type 22mm diameter rising main the tee must be a 22mm size reducing to 15mm.)

A tap kit is a much more convenient arrangement to fit, if your water authority allows it – most now do. It contains everything you need to make the installation, except a length of extension pipe to reach the break-in point.

A typical kit consists of: stopvalve, pipe clips, push-fit tee, brass wall elbow, pliable copper pipe (to fit through the wall), and plastic tap with hose nozzle. Most suppliers also stock lengths of 15mm polybutylene (plastic) pipe, which you can substitute for copper pipe.

Automatic supply connectors are available, which replace the standard tee. The device is clamped over the pipe and a small charge inside, when activated, will pierce the mains pipe.

Planning the installation

Before you buy the components for your new tap, consider what the installation involves. Siting the tap where it will be most convenient in use is your priority. If you need it at the front and back of the house, position it where it's accessible to both areas, using a hose. Aim to locate the tap over a drainage gully (or at least a paved area) to cope with the inevitable spillage; avoid flower beds and grass or you'll soon form a mud patch.

The tap should be connected into the

Opposite *Light the great outdoors and extend your gardening time: power the shed or outhouse worktop, or simply illuminate the garden for use in those summertime evenings.*

A garden tap makes watering the garden so much more convenient – comprehensive kits in plastic make the installation a simple, quick and satisfying job.

outer leaf. Which ever method you use, wear stout gloves and goggles as protection against flying fragments. Test-fit a length of 15mm copper pipe in the hole.

Connecting to the rising main
So that you can work out the various lengths of pipework needed to complete the run it's best to tee into the rising main first. If you're using a conventional compression or capillary fitting, or a pushfit tee, you'll have to drain down the rising main. Turn off the main stop valve and open the kitchen cold tap to drain off the water.

Mark a cutting line on the pipe and saw through it, absolutely squarely, using a junior hacksaw (place a bowl under the pipe to catch any remaining water in the pipe). Measure from the cut the width of the tee piece. Allow for the amount that's to be slotted inside at each end (measure the depth of the internal pipe stop) then make a second cut to remove the section of pipe. File off the burrs inside and outside the cut ends and (for compression fittings) bevel the edges slightly.

To fit a compression tee, slip its capnuts onto the pipe ends, then the soft copper 'olives' (which compress to form the seal). Insert the tee fitting – you'll need to release the pipe from its brackets for fitting clearance – and tighten up the capnuts, using an adjustable spanner.

To fit a capillary tee, polish the pipe ends with wire wool then apply flux by brush. Insert the tee, then place a heat-proof board (an asbestos iron stand will do) behind the joint. Play the flame of a blowtorch over one of the joints until you see a ring of solder appear around the mouth of the fitting. Leave the joint to cool, the repeat for the other joint. Wrap a wet cloth round the first joint to prevent the solder melting again.

A plastic push-fit tee is simple to fit: just apply silicone lubricant (or washing-up liquid) to the pipe ends and inside the fitting, then slot it into the pipe run.

By far the easiest way to tap into the rising main is to use an automatic connector. Simply clamp the device to the pipe (don't even turn off the water) and leave until the rest of the pipe run is assembled and you're ready to make the connection.

Assembling the branch pipe
Fit the pipe in the exit hole: with compression or capillary fittings you'll need to fit an elbow at each end; with pliable copper just hand-bend it in the direction of the supply.

To use conventional plumbing, measure between the exit pipe and the tee fitting and cut a length of 15mm copper pipe to fit.

rising main for maximum water pressure, and the position of this pipe will influence where you run the new branch. You'll be able to identify the main: the kitchen sink's cold tap is fed directly from it, whether you've a direct system (all fixtures fed directly from the main) or an indirect one (fixtures – except the kitchen tap – fed from a cold water tank).

Once you've found where to break into the rising main, trace a route (the least conspicuous one) to your tap position.

Running a pipe through a wall
Mark the wall outside where the tap is to go: it can be any convenient height above the ground, so long as there's room for a bucket underneath and you don't have to stoop to use it. Use a reference point common to inside and outside (a window or door frame for instance) and transfer the tap position to the wall indoors, using a tape measure, try square or spirit level as a guide.

You can cut through the wall with a club hammer and long cold chisel but it's easier to use an electric hammer drill fitted with a large-diameter masonry bit. Unless you have a drill with an extension piece you'll have to form the hole from both sides: on a solid wall drill about 110mm (4¾in) then go outside and complete the hole: on a cavity wall continue until the drill bit breaks through the inner leaf, then repeat for the

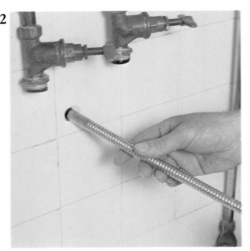

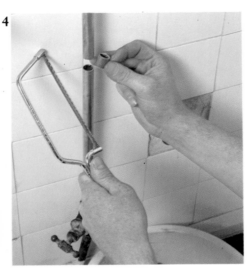

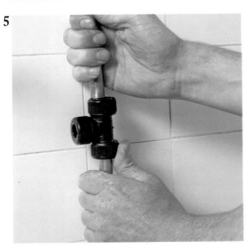

1. *Drill a hole through the outside wall to take the water supply pipe.*
2. *Use hand-bendable copper pipe as the exit pipe – it's available in convenient lengths to suit most walls.*
3. *Drain down the rising main and break into it by fitting a tee connector – a plastic push-fit fitting is the simplest to use. First mark its position on the pipe.*
4. *Cut out the section of rising main using a hacksaw, then prepare the pipe ends by deburring and lubricating ready for the connector tee.*
5. *Slot the push-fit tee onto the ends of the cut rising main – you don't have to dismantle these fittings to make a good, watertight seal, although you may need sufficient play in the pipe to enable the connection to be made.*
6. *Fit a stopcock to the end of the bendable exit pipe – it's necessary to isolate the garden supply during the winter, when bursts could occur.*

Allow for the insertion of a stop valve in this run. Assemble the run with compression or capillary fittings, as previously described, and secure the pipe to special brackets.

Outside you may need to fit a short vertical run to the tap location. Assemble this and attach an angled tap connector incorporating a wall bracket to the end. Fit an inclined bib tap with compression fittings.

To assemble a push-fit pipe run, lubricate the end of the pliable copper exit pipe and slot on the plastic stop valve. Fit a pipe clip to the wall and clip the pipe in place. Measure between the stop valve and the tee fitting on the rising main, allowing for the amount of pipe to be inserted in each end. You can use flexible polybutylene pipe for this run. It's sold in various sized reels or lengths for fitting to size: even if the run is especially long you won't need to join

7. *Measure between the stopcock and the rising main tee connector, cut a length of pipe to fit, then slot it in place.*
8. *Outside, screw a brass wall plate and elbow to the end of the exit pipe, using the compression fittings.*
9. *Screw the plastic bib tap onto the elbow fitting, set it upright, then fit the optional hose nozzle. Mount the hose nearby for convenience.*

sections and the pipe can cope with fairly tight bends, too. Cut the pipe squarely with a hacksaw, deburr the ends and lubricate. Insert the special metal inserts supplied into each end then slot the pipe into the tee and stopvalve connections. Make sure to clip the pipe to the wall at intervals.

Outside, bend the pliable pipe downwards to the tap position and connect a compression wall elbow to its end. Screw the elbow into wall plugs, then screw the plastic bib tap into its socket. Wind some PTFE sealing tape onto the screw thread first to make a good seal and so you can fit the tap vertically. Seal the gap between wall and exit pipe with mastic.

Restore the water supply (make sure the new tap is off) and check the system for leaks. To activate an automatic connector, remove the device's plastic firing pin cap and strike the firing pin sharply with a hammer. A loud crack signals that the charge inside has pierced the rising main.

Fitting a second garden tap
A second tap is a real boon to gardening. Site it at the far end of a long plot for best effect. To make the connection, insert a tee fitting (compression or push-fit only) in the outside vertical section of the exit pipe (you'll need a special pliable pipe with an unridged mid-piece for this) and run a length of 12mm polythene or plastic pipe to the second tap position. Bury the pipe about 500mm (1ft 8in) underground in a trench, out of harm's way. At the other end, connect the pipe to a standpipe – a vertical length of pipe fixed to a stout post or to the wall of an outbuilding. Attach the second bib tap as previously described.

Watering the garden
All plants and crops demand water to survive but often nature is lax in supplying it in sufficient quantity and it's up to the gardener to make up the balance. But knowing just how much water to administer, and when, is quite another matter.

When to water
Watering is probably most important between the months of April and September, when the plants are growing and the sun is at is strongest. Nevertheless, this depends on the rainfall in your area: some regions receive too much, others too little.

Aspect is a deciding factor (a north-facing site will dry out less quickly than one facing south), and soil type (see page 12) should also be considered (clay soil holds more water than sandy soil, yet each has its particular problems).

In short there is no simple answer, but there are priorities. Newly-planted trees, shrubs, and other plants, and of course seedlings, are high on the priority list. Among the vegetables, crops like peas and beans will give a much better yield if they don't go short of water, and radishes need plenty of moisture if they are not to go woody. Soft fruits, too, such as black currants, raspberries, and strawberries will give a much better crop if they are watered while the fruit is developing.

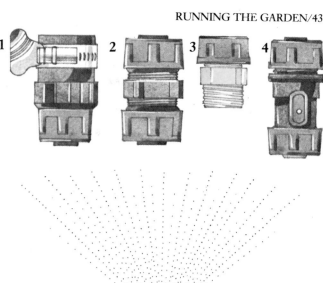

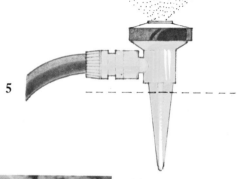

Lawns will turn brown if not watered, but they will grow again when wet weather returns. If you start to water the lawn, you will have to water heavily and frequently to keep it green.

Whatever you water, do so thoroughly even if it means less frequently. Lots of light sprinklings can encourage detrimental surface rooting.

Greenhouse watering

While a garden tap (see pages 38–42) will permit hand-watering of greenhouse plants, automated systems take over the chore from you. The two principal systems depend on either capillary action from special mats or a sand base, or on a drip feed from individual nozzles. In either case they can be fed down hand-filled reservoirs, or by mains-fed cisterns.

Equipment for garden watering

A lightweight, capacious watering can is a basic need: choose one with a long spout fixed near the base in 7–9 litre (1½–2 gallon) capacity.

An adaptable hosepipe can be used on its own or in conjunction with numerous nozzles. Choose a long enough one for the job. Although some are inexpensive it is probably worth paying more for a reinforced plastic hosepipe; they are stronger and easier to handle. Unkinkable and flat-packed types are available.

As a hose attachment, a sprinkler is an ideal way to apply water over a period of time. Numerous models with oscillating, pulsating or rotating heads are made; choice will be affected by the size of the plot, the water pressure, and cost.

Above left *A selection of garden watering equipment, including perforated hose, and (clockwise from left) rotating sprinkler, watering-can hose attachment, a large rotating sprinkler, a star-shaped disc sprinkler and an oscillating sprinkler.*
1. *tap connector*
2. *hose connector*
3. *sprinkler connector*
4. *on/off connector*
5. *spiked mini sprinkler, which covers a small circular area*

Garden hygiene

A messy garden is unsightly and unhealthy. Sickly plants and decaying debris, if allowed to remain, will encourage pests and diseases. An unkempt greenhouse, too, can harbour disease. To eradicate these unsavoury elements, you need to know just what they are, where they come from, and where they lurk. Once you have identified the cause, cure is just a matter of an orderly and extremely meticulous work routine.

Pests and diseases

Trouble can come to your garden in many different ways.

Weeds can act as host to both pests and diseases, besides looking untidy and competing for nutrients. Keep your garden weed-free, then it will look nicer and the plants are likely to be healthier (the pests and diseases will still attack your plants, but they will be easier to keep under control if there is not present and flourishing infection and infestation already within the garden).

Sickly-looking plants should be viewed with suspicion, especially if they have mottled, yellowish, or crinkled leaves. These symptoms could be due to other causes, but virus diseases are likely causes. These are particularly troublesome because they cannot be controlled with sprays, but are likely to be spread to other plants of the same kind by sap-sucking insects such as aphids. If a plant looks very sickly and you just can't track the problem down to an obvious pest or disease, you must be drastic and burn it.

Diseases can also be carried on fallen leaves and rotting debris. Some fungus diseases such as botrytis may start on dead tissue but spread to healthy growth; dead leaves may also contain other harmful fungus spores (rose leaves may sometimes contain those spores that cause the black spot disease for instance).

Play safe, sweep up or pick up fallen petals and leaves, and, preferably, burn them.

Disposing of crop remains

The remains of vegetable crops are easy to dispose of, so long as they're free from disease. In the autumn, simply chop through what's left of the growth with a sharp spade, and dig into the soil. This will form a green manure that adds humus to the soil (see pages 13–15). Tough roots, or the roots of perenials that are likely to grow again, should be removed and burnt or composted. Alternatively, you can put all undiseased crop remains on your compost heap (see pages 13–15).

Sterile conditions

Soil conditioning, regular weeding, watering and feeding, coupled with general garden hygiene, is the best way to ensure a healthy plot. But the water and the compost that you use to encourage your plants to grow could actually carry pests or diseases.

The water you give to your plants and crops should be uncontaminated. And the worst source of contaminated water is the water butt. The belief that rainwater gathered in a butt from the roof is good for plants is misguided. Although it does not contain the lime that can be a problem for some plants in some areas, it is likely to have a good population of pests and diseases, as well as dead leaves and other debris.

Your safest bet is to use tap water for glass-grown plants and save the contents of the water butt for the more hardy specimens outside. Only a few greenhouse plants will resent hard tap water, but you can make special arrangements for these.

Always try to use sterilized compost for pot plants (some peat-based composts may not be sterilized but because the peat is unlikely to be contaminated, these are perfectly saftisfactory). Once the bags are opened, keep the top of the bag folded over, or transfer the compost to a clean plastic dustbin with a lid, which you can keep in the greenhouse or shed.

Most commercial methods of soil sterilization are not suitable for the amateur, but if the soil needs to be sterilized (outdoors or in the greenhouse) you could treat it with a solution of formalin (which you may be able to buy at a garden centre). Late winter or early spring is the best time for this job. First clear the soil, then dilute the formalin and use strictly according to the instructions on the container. (Avoid inhaling the fumes: they're pungent and irritating.)

Use a watering can with a rose to sprinkle the solution generously and evenly on the soil, which should be moist. Cover the area with sheets of polythene anchored with

Below *Chop through disease-free crops with a spade and turn them into the soil to form a green manure that adds beneficial humus to the soil.*

Bottom *Burn tough roots, the roots of perennials and other growths that are likely to grow again or cause obstructions.*

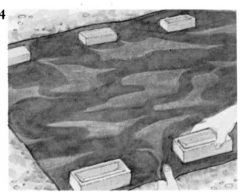

1. *Dig up any plants you want to save, plus crop remains, then break up large lumps in the soil. Water until moist but not sodden.*
2. *Dilute formalin with water according to the instructions on the bottle, and stir the solution well.*
3. *Sprinkle the formalin solution onto the soil from a watering can fitted with a rose; aim to drench the soil thoroughly.*
4. *Cover the treated area with sheets of black polythene held down with bricks to retain the fumes.*
5. *Two days later, uncover the soil and dig to release the fumes. Don't use the soil for three weeks.*
6. *Sterilize plant pots by immersing them in formalin solution for 48 hours, then wash thoroughly. Don't use clay pots for one week after sterilizing.*

bricks at the edges, to contain the fumes. Leave for two days. Remove the sheets and lightly dig over the soil to release all the fumes. Don't use the soil for three weeks (outdoors) or six weeks (indoors).

You can also sterilize pots, tools and other garden equipment by immersing them for two days in formalin solution, after which you should wash them thoroughly. Leave clay pots for a week before using.

Steam sterilization is the most effective method of treating your greenhouse soil, though as its unlikely that you have access to equipment to sterilize it *in situ*, it can be a tedius job to excavate it and replace it in small batches.

The soil temperature should be rapidly raised to about 82°C (180°F) and held there for about 15 minutes. Proprietary steamers are available, but it's easy to make your own – but be warned, unless the temperature and the timing are right you

can actually be more harmful and leave the soil in a worse condition than before. There are complex biological and chemical reactions involved that can upset nutrient availability and even inhibit the normal germination and growth.

For very small amounts of soil, you can simply boil 300ml (½pt) water in a large saucepan and add soil to within 12mm (½in) of the rim. Put on the lid and simmer for about 15 minutes, then turn out on a clean surface for a while to completely cool down.

For larger quantities of soil, use a clean oil drum with a lid. Put the soil in the drum, inside a hessian sack, add about 50mm (2in) of water and boil rapidly to produce steam for about 20 minutes. The sack must be suspended over the water on a rod spanning the drum. A camping gas stove is the ideal medium to heat up the water in the garden.

Fumigating the greenhouse

Pests and diseases can lurk within the framework of the greenhouse, and fumigation is a good way to eradicate them. There are various chemicals sold for greenhouse fumigation, so be clear about their uses – and check which plants are likely to be damaged and therefore need removing first. In the case of sulphur fumigation, all plants must be removed.

If the greenhouse is empty, you could try the old method of burning flowers of sulphur or special sulphur candles (sometimes sold by garden centres and horticultural specialists). Position the candles or flowers of sulphur centrally, light, following the manufacturer's instructions, and vacate the greenhouse, closing the door behind you. Don't re-enter until the following day, when the fumes will have dispersed. You can safely return your plants shortly after.

You may find the various modern insecticides or fungicidal smoke cones or pellets more convenient to use. With these you actually control the pests and diseases on the plants as well as the structure, and there is no need to remove the plants (other than any that the instructions say are not suitable for treatment).

Burning garden refuse

Any garden refuse that you can't use on your compost heap should be burned. The potash that's produced can be added to the soil to improve its fertility (keep the ash dry until you are ready to use it).

A bonfire is a good way to dispose of unwanted rubbish but you must take care to build it properly and use it safely. Your aim should be to make a bonfire that burns rather than smokes – a smoky fire is a nuisance to neighbours and a health hazard. Make a cone of dry wood or crumple some wire and use this as the heart of the bonfire, to ensure the necessary updraught of air in the centre. Add only dry material to the pile. Never pour petrol or any inflammable substance on the fire – if it's slow to start, use crumpled newspaper or fire lighters.

An incinerator will contain small amounts of refuse while it's burning. Various types are made, from an expanded metal mesh box on legs to a steel-framed container with

1. *A proprietary steel-framed incinerator with riddle attachment to shake out the ashes.*
2. *A contained dustbin incinerator with lid and chimney provides the neatest way to dispose of rubbish.*
3. *An expanded metal mesh incinerator in a steel, legged frame.*

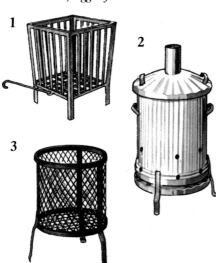

riddle base and the metal dustbin incinerator complete with chimney. When buying an incinerator, choose one with thick walls, as thin material will not withstand the intense, prolonged heat for long.

You can build your own incinerator from concrete building blocks laid without mortar. Construct a basic box shape with gaps between each block for air passage. Pile scrap piping in the base as a grate.

Electricity outdoors

Taking electricity outdoors will extend the use of your garden immensely. Whether you turn your shed into a workshop by installing sockets for power tools and appliances, bring light and heat to the greenhouse, or simply dispense with a trailing extension lead when using an electric lawnmower, you'll discover how adaptable your plot becomes. If your preferences are for far more relaxing activities, power for pool lights and pumps, illumination for the patio, complete the picture.

Before you even contemplate running a supply outside, consider what's involved. Electricity can kill, if misused. Outside, there's greater risk of fittings getting wet (electricity and water are a lethal combination) and the installation is more exposed to physical damage, from garden tools for example. In short, pay particular heed to the very stringent rules governing outdoor electricity supplies. Whatever you do must comply with the IEE (Institute of Electrical Engineers) wiring regulations, and above all *never* attempt any electrical work unless you're confident and thoroughly competent. If you're at all unsure, abandon the project and call in a qualified electrician.

Types of installation

Sensible precautions apart, an electrical supply outdoors is quite straightforward to arrange. There are basically four options open to you:
● A socket mounted externally on the house wall, which can be connected to an existing inside circuit.
● Lighting and socket outlets in a greenhouse, shed or detached garage, for which you'll need to provide a separate circuit, taken from a spare fuseway in the consumer unit (fusebox) or via a new switchfuse unit, complete with isolating switch.
● Waterproof sockets mounted on sturdy posts in the garden, using a separate circuit.
● Garden lighting and a supply for a pool pump run from a low-voltage supply, connected to a transformer, or a mains supply.

Separate circuits can be buried underground, carried overhead or fixed to a boundary wall (but *not* a fence; it could be blown over in a high wind). Armoured PVC cable and MICC (mineral insulated copper covered) cable made specially for outdoor use are available, but call for special tools to connect them up.

You could use ordinary PVC-sheathed two-core-and-earth cable through heavy-duty conduits or pipe if it runs underground (plastic conduit is available with various push-fit, solvent-weld connectors); an overhead cable must be (unbroken) at least 3.5m (11ft 6in) above the ground (5.2m/17ft over a drive) and supported by sturdy posts. If the span is more than 3.5m (11ft 6in) a catenary wire must be used to support the cable.

It's acceptable to use ordinary plastic sockets in the greenhouse or shed but impact-resistant, or metal-clad boxes are more resilient to knocks. In a greenhouse, especially, where there is a lot of moisture, it is wise to use a special greenhouse control panel. Externally, you will need to fit a metal-clad socket that's has a special waterproof casing.

All outdoor circuits must be protected against potentially lethal faults. A normal fuse or MCB (miniature circuit breaker) isn't sufficient: not only would it be too slow to react to some faults and 'blow', but also there are some faults it wouldn't even sense. You must fit a high sensitivity residual current device (RCD), sometimes called a current operated earth-leakage circuit breaker (ELCB) · *in addition to* a circuit fuse or MCB.

The RCD will 'trip' and isolate the circuit when it senses a fault current as low as 30mA – and that's well below the level of a fatal shock. For a normal 30A outdoor circuit, use an RCD rated at 30A.

Socket on a house wall

A single socket fitted on the exterior wall of your house is ideal if you have a small garden. There are two ways to connect the socket to the house wiring:
● **To an existing ring main power circuit.** Connect a length of 2.5mm² two-core-and-earth cable directly to the back of an existing socket on the circuit (the socket must be on the ring main and *not* already on a spur) and run this branch to the new socket. Alternatively, you can break into the ring main (not a spur cable), install a three-terminal junction box and run your new branch from here to the new socket. The ring main and its spurs cannot serve an area greater than 100m².
● **To a radial circuit.** Connect a cable to any socket on the radial circuit and run it to the new socket. A circuit wired in 2.5mm² cable and fused at 20A can serve only

A well-lit garden patio enables you to sit out on warm summer evenings and makes the most of your garden.

1. *To fit a socket on a house wall, drill through the masonry using a large-diameter bit. Drill from both sides.*
2. *Fit plastic conduit from the break out point to the socket location, then fit a special outside socket.*
3. *Feed the electric cable through the conduit from inside the house, then trim and strip the cable cores.*
4. *Connect the cable cores to the terminals of the faceplate, making sure they're not strained.*
5. *Fit the socket faceplate to the body then fit the weatherproof cover when you're not using the socket.*
6. *Fit an ELCB between the fuse and the consumer unit to protect the entire house from danger if a fault develops.*

20m²; one wired in 4mm² cable and fused at 30A can serve only 50mm².

Choose a suitable location on the wall for the new socket and work out the easiest route to the connection point. The socket should be about 1.2m (4ft) above the ground: you may decide to run the cable up the wall to a first floor circuit, down to a ground floor one, or directly back through the wall in order to run the cable mainly inside.

Drill a downward-sloping hole through the wall, from inside (to prevent moisture trickling in), using a masonry bit that matches the diameter of a length of plastic conduit – this is to prevent the cable from chafing.

Insert the conduit, then run a length of cable through. Attach an elbow connector to direct the conduit up or down (if necessary) and add a length of conduit to reach the socket location. Fit a conduit adaptor in the socket mounting box, attach the box to the wall with screws and plugs (fixing into the bricks, not the mortar) then feed in the cable. Strip and connect the cores of the cable to the socket's terminals (red to live; black to neutral; green/yellow to earth), then fit the faceplate.

Run the cable to the break-in point, clipping it to the sides of the joists at 500mm (20in) intervals (or run it through holes drilled halfway down the joists if the route is at right-angles to them). Where the cable runs along the wall, fit it in plastic mini-trunking for neatness. Now you can connect into the power circuit.

Before you go any further, switch off the power at the mains, or remove the relevant circuit fuse or MCB. Test a socket to ensure it's dead.

If you're taking a spur from a power socket, unscrew the socket's faceplate and pull it gently forward. Feed in the new branch cable, strip the cores and connect red to live; black to neutral; and green/yellow to earth. Sleeve the earth core with green/yellow striped PVC. Replace the faceplate and restore the power.

To connect into the ring main via a junction box, cut the power cable at the point as close to the proposed new socket as possible, ideally where it runs along a joist. Screw a 30A three-terminal junction box to the joist. Connect up the cable cores to the relevant terminals (sleeve the earth core) then run in the new branch cable from the new socket. Fit the junction box cover, then restore the power.

With this type of installation it's possible to fit a 'socket outlet RCD' on the outside wall. This is a unit the size of a double socket, but containing one outlet and its own RCD. It will protect just that socket – particularly beneficial to anyone using a power tool from it.

Adding a new circuit

If you're running a completely new circuit outdoors there are two ways you can do this:
● Connect the new circuit cable to a spare fuseway in the consumer unit. If the spare fuseway isn't of the correct rating for the circuit, buy a new fuse or MCB of the correct rating and fit this in the consumer unit in the correct position (highest rating should be nearest the unit's isolating switch).
● If there's no spare fuseway, install a new switchfuse unit (really a small consumer unit) next to the existing one, and connect the new circuit cable to it. Call in the electricity board to disconnect the meter tails and reconnect them, and those from thé new unit, via a 'distribution box'. This is because only two tails can actually enter the meter.

Running cable underground

Burying the new cable run is the neatest, least conspicuous method. Plan out the route first, then mark it out with string and pegs. Choose the shortest route, but avoid paths, intervening walls, flower beds and the vegetable patch (or anywhere there's likely to be deep-digging).

Dig a trench about 500mm (20in) deep × 100mm (4in) wide and add a 25mm (1in) thick layer of sand to the bottom if the ground is particularly stony. Cut a length of cable (you'll need 6mm² two-core-and-earth cable for a 30A supply) to run from the switchgear at one end of the circuit to that at the oppostie end. Thread the cable through lengths of heavy-duty plastic conduit and assemble the sections, using solvent weld adhesive. You'll need to fit

1. *Dig a trench for the new cable run, leading from the house to the outbuilding. Shovel sand in the base of the trench.*
2. *Fit the cable in conduit buried in the base of the trench, then cover with a brick or stone to prevent accidental damage when digging in the future.*

elbow connectors at each end to run the cable vertically out of the ground and into the house and outbuilding.

Drill a hole and pass the cable through the wall, as previously described.

If there's a wall connecting the house with the outbuilding, run the cable along this (encased in conduit) instead of burying it. In the trench, cover the conduit with a protective roof ridge tile or slab. Don't fill in the trench until you've tested the new circuit.

Running cable overhead

Although running your new circuit cable overhead isn't as neat as an underground installation, it could be the answer if your garden is substantially paved or the route to the outbuilding especially long.

On spans up to 3m (10ft) you can fix up ordinary 6mm² twin-and-earth PVC cable without additional support, but on longer spans it must be strung onto a catenary wire, which is tensioned between an eyebolt and straining screw. At the outbuilding you'll probably have to erect a stout post to attach the incoming supply cable to. Set a length of preservative-treated 100 × 50mm (4 × 2in) sawn timber in concrete as for fixing a fence post (see pages 26–27). Attach an eye bolt to the house wall and fix the catenary wire to it.

At the outbuilding, secure the turnbuckle to a second eye bolt, attach the catenary wire (which should be cut under-length) then tighten the buckle, using a pair of screwdrivers, to strain the wire.

Attach the circuit cable (remember to cut it over-length by about 300mm/12in as it will sag in the middle). Hang the cable from the wire on cable ties at roughly 500mm (20in) intervals, with loops between each so rainwater will drip off. Make a drip loop at each end before taking the cable through the

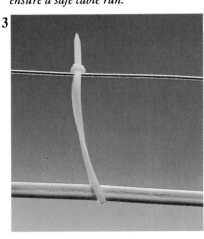

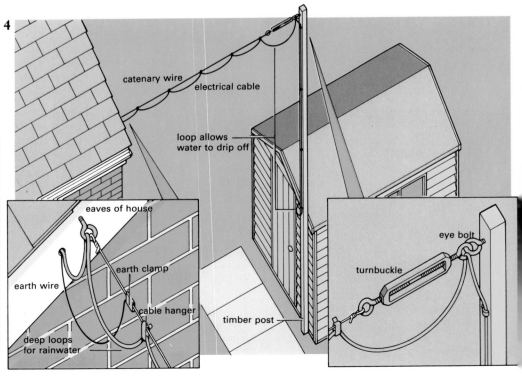

1. *Overhead cable must be supported by a catenary wire. First attach the earth wire to its clamp.*
2. *Rig up the catenary with a turnbuckle at one end to place sufficient strain on the wire.*
3. *String the cable between plastic cable ties, with loops between each so rainwater will drip off.*
4. *The overhead set-up between house and outbuilding, showing all connections you'll need to make to ensure a safe cable run.*

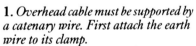

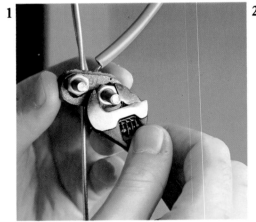

catenary wire

electrical cable

loop allows water to drip off

eaves of house

earth clamp

earth wire

cable hanger

deep loops for rainwater

timber post

eye bolt

turnbuckle

wall. The catenary wire must be earthed, using a separate green/yellow sheathed length of 6mm² single-core earth cable to run it to the connection point indoors.

Connections in the outbuilding

The connections you make in the out-building depend on what facilities you require.

To power just a few socket outlets and a light, connect the cores of your radial power circuit direct to a small switchfuse unit containing two fuses or MCBs. Run cables to lights and socket outlets, but be careful you don't exceed the 30A current provision or you'll have to fit larger supply cable, RCDs and main fuses of MCBs. A smaller installation only requires one 30A fuseway: you can feed a light circuit via a 5A fused connection unit.

Under recent wiring regulations, the new switchfuse unit must be fitted with an ELCB (see page 47) to provide extra protection to anyone operating a power tool outdoors run from the new socket, unless the circuit is already so protected.

Connections in the house

To provide power to your new circuit, connect the length of cable to the mains. Remember, before starting this part of the job, to switch off at the mains and don't switch back on again until you're sure everything is in working order.

Run the cable to the consumer unit. If you're connecting it direct to a spare fuseway, strip the cores and secure in the relevant terminals (remembering to sleeve the earth core). If you aren't installing an RCD to protect the entire house and outside installation as previously described, you must fit a device in the new cable run near the consumer unit.

Low-voltage power

Garden lights, underwater pool lights and pumps to power a fountain or waterfall can have either a low-voltage or direct mains supply.

With the former, a step-down transformer is used: place it inside the house or outbuilding, and run a length of special low-voltage cable to the pump or appliance. Although it's not vital to bury this cable (you wouldn't receive a fatal shock from it) it's best to insert it in conduit or a length of hosepipe for protection, and ideally to put it in a trench out of harm's way. To provide power, simply plug the transformer's flex into a spare 13A socket.

With mains supply, the pump cable is connected to a length of 0.5mm² two-core-and-earth flex run underground in conduit: the connection must be made with a heavy-duty waterproof three-pin connector, which should be firmly housed in a waterproof compartment near the pool side. The other end of the flex must be connected to a three-pin plug and inserted in a 13A socket. As an extra safety precaution, substitute the ordinary plug for a plug-in RCD (rated at 30mA and fused at 2A); it's wired up in exactly the same way as a conventional type of plug.

Ring or radial?

House power sockets are wired on a 'ring' or 'radial' circuit. You can add a spur to a ring or radial circuit socket only where no other spur has been added. So any socket with three cables entering it will already have a spur linked to it, and so cannot be used.

But telling the difference between sockets with two cables requires further investigation. In the past, spurs could have one double or two single sockets. Now only one outlet per spur is permitted. So if the socket has two cables, it could be a ring socket, the intermediate socket on an old two-outlet spur, or an intermediate socket on the old radial circuit.

To check whether a socket is on a ring circuit or not, you will need a 'continuity tester', which you can make from a 4 volt battery, a length of twin bell wire and a torch bulb. Connect the cores of the wire to the battery terminals. Then connect the bulb into just one core.

Turn off the mains current. Disconnect the live (red) cores from the socket terminals and touch the tester leads to the cores. The bulb will light if the socket is on a ring; it will stay out if it's on a radial circuit or spur. If it's a ring, you can add a spur. To discover whether the socket is a spur or on a radial circuit, trace the cables from the socket back to a ring socket and onto a socket with only one cable, then you have a spur: don't extend from the intermediate socket. If you trace the cables back to the consumer unit and looping on to more than one socket, it's a radial circuit: you can extend it (so long as the circuit doesn't serve an area greater than 20sq m/215sq ft and is wired in 2.5m² cable).

If you find these instructions complicated, or do not feel confident, call in professional advice.

CHAPTER 4
FRUIT CAGES & PLANT SUPPORTS

Your garden is under threat of constant attack by birds, rodents and the unpredicatable force of the elements. Each can decimate your prize crops unless you take preventative action to protect the plot.

Unless you're wary, your garden will fall prey to numerous destructive influences. Pesticides and insecticides will cope with a large part of the problem, but there are, unfortunately, some far more determined culprits.

Birds are, in many ways, the gardener's allies: some of them consume slugs, harmful insects, and other pests that can terrorize your plot. Unfortunately our feathered friends lose favour with budding fruit growers because of their predilection for eating ripening crops. During the winter they make themselves a nuisance by pecking out the dormant blossom buds. In both cases you could find yourself sporting a fruitless fruit tree. If you've an established tree, or you're planning a mini-orchard, you should take steps to prevent birds from reaching your trees at these vulnerable times, or make provision to at least scare them off.

Vegetable gardeners can be equally frustrated by birds that eat the seeds before they germinate, or possibly seriously damage growing crops (wood pigeons are a particular problem).

Bird barriers

Repellent sprays are not really a viable proposition, because the chemicals need frequent applications when they're washed off by rain. What's needed is a physical deterrent, and there are various types you can employ.

Some bird barriers are basic in the extreme. Stringing bushes and trees with ordinary black cotton is usually an effective way to protect your fruit, but don't form a complex grid: just a few strands will suffice and eventually a bird will find it and flee. Onlooking birds will get the message, too, though some birds soon get used to cotton and are quite happy to hop around it. Don't use unbreakable nylon threads, however; the object is not to inflict any unpleasant injury on the birds.

You can buy special ultra-fine white rayon webbing in hanks from garden centres, which is ideal for draping over bushes or protecting fruit buds and ripening tree fruits, which are prone to attack. The web won't trap the hapless bird but scares it off and the material rots after a few months and disperses.

Assuming your trees have escaped attack until their fruits have formed, you have to prepare for further attacks. Safeguard individual fruits (peaches and nectarines, for instance) by wrapping them in muslin or alternatively polythene bags. If you use the latter, be sure to puncture the bags for essential ventilation. Don't make the holes too big otherwise you won't be able to ward off another flying fruit menace: the wasp. Old nylon stockings or cut up tights, also come in handy for enclosing particularly susceptible fruit.

Where you can't protect individual fruit (on a currant bush, for example) you can drape the entire bush, if it's fairly compact, with a square of 19–25mm (¾–1in) cotton or nylon mesh netting, staked to the ground all round. This treatment is ideal for protecting strawberries during their brief cropping season. Most netting – even nylon – will rot or deteriorate after exposure to

Opposite *With care and attention, superb crops, unblemished by birds and pests, can be grown.*

the weather and the sun, so treat this type of cover as a temporary safegard.

Cage your fruit

It's advisable to keep the netting clear of the fruit, so you can erect temporary cages over fruit bushes and plants and small trees by lashing together a framework of bamboo canes and driving the uprights into the ground. Drape netting over the framework and stake at the base. Protect the netting from snagging on the canes at the corners by extending the uprights by about 50mm (2in) and upending a jam-jar on top of each, so the net will hang smoothly on the rounded jars.

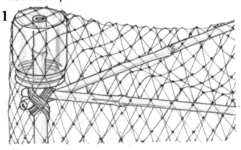

Proprietary cage systems are available; the most popular one has durable solid rubber balls pierced with six holes. Simply slot metal rods into the holes to form the frame, and attach intermediate rods with more balls, as well as at the corners.

Aluminium rods, 12mm (½in) in diameter and in 600mm–2.4m (2–8ft) lengths are sold for the purpose of fruit cage construction.

Fruit trees grown against a wall can easily be protected. Simply hang netting like a curtain over the trees, supported on a timber frame.

For the more enthusiastic fruit-grower, you'll probably find it advantageous to grow all your fruit trees and bushes together on one large plot and to cover the entire area with a large, permanent cage. Proprietary fruit cages are available, using sturdy

aluminium alloy, galvanized steel or plasticized tubular steel as the frames. Most types are sold in a range of useful sizes and can be assembled easily by slotting the components together. Be sure to choose a size that covers all your crops and allows you to work comfortably inside.

Secure the netting to the top horizontal cross-rails using special net hooks (you'll probably be given a supply of these with the cage) and stake at the bottom with ground pins.

There may be a metal-framed door included in the cage set-up but do be sure it's sufficiently wide to admit your wheelbarrow. A doorway isn't vital, as a generous flap in the netting secured with tape or clips will serve the same purpose.

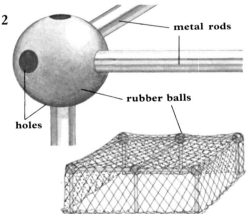

Be sure to remove the roof netting from your cage when the birds aren't likely to peck the fruit or buds, so that they can busy themselves with their more helpful task of eating all the harmful insects, grubs and eggs. You'd be wise to remove the netting in the event of a heavy fall of snow: snow can soon build up on a net, causing it to sag onto the trees and possibly tear. Far worse, the considerable weight could even demolish the entire cage and damage your crops.

If you'd rather opt for the homemade approach, there's no reason why you can't build a substantial fruit cage yourself. Choose fairly stout, perhaps 50mm square (2in sq), preservative-treated softwood for

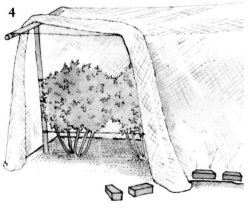

1. *Home-made cage.*
2. *Proprietary cage system.*
3. *Large, permanent cage.*
4. *Large, home-made cage for large fruit trees.*

Below *Protect wall fruit, such as these pears, by supporting netting on wooden frames.*

Above *Protecting your shrubs and fruit trees helps to keep rodents at bay.*

Left *A sturdy prefabricated fruit cage will protect your delicate crops from the attentions of even the most persistent pests.*

Below left *You can make your cage, tailored to suit the shape, size and style of your garden, using stout timber frames with netting to keep out all the greedy pests.*

the cage uprights, firmly fixed into the ground, with horizontal cross-rails screwed or skew-nailed to their tops. Thinner diagonal braces may be necessary to make a rigid frame. Fix the netting as normal to the top rails and stake to the ground.

Rodents on the rampage

Birds aren't the only hoards with an eye on your fruit trees. Squirrels, rabbits, and hares may be frequent visitors to your orchards, and they often display cunning to bypass your defences. Squirrels have been

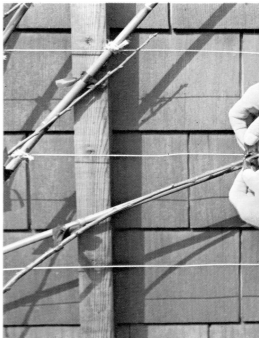

Above *Squirrels are fairly cunning when it comes to a tasty treat, and have been known to lift netting to reach ripe crops – take into account their stealth when you build your fruit cage.*

Top right *The branches of a fan-trained tree being tied to canes, which are fixed to the wires of a wall mounted support.*

Right *Espaliers, cordons and fan-trained trees can be grown on a system of horizontal wires strung between straining posts.*

Opposite *To grow wire-trained trees away from a wall, erect a frame of horizontal wires stretched between vertical wooden posts set in the ground. You'll need to add a diagonal brace to the end posts. Use straining bolts held in the end post to adjust the tension of the wires. The wires are fastened to the intermediate posts with staples, which are just hammered in.*

known to lift the netting and scramble beneath, while rabbits tend to prefer digging a tunnel to gain access.

One solution is to set 1.2m (4ft) wide, 25mm (1in) mesh wire-netting about 300mm (1ft) deep in the ground at the perimeter of the fruit-growing area, even the entire garden. Bend out the bottom of the netting to frustrate burrowing.

As a second line of defence, use perforated plastic rodent protectors or cylinder of mesh wire-netting wrapped around the base of each fruit tree (about 1m/3ft high) to fend off intruders. This also wards against the menace of cats sharpening their claws on the trunks.

Battling with the elements
Animals and birds may be deterred fairly easily from ravaging your garden but defending the plot against the elements is quite another matter. While efficient garden drainage (see pages 10–11) will cope with the problems associated with heavy rainfall, the effects of wind and frost requires special attention.

Young trees, newly planted, for example, can be blown over even by fairly moderate winds, especially if frost combines the attack and loosens the roots before they can establish a foothold in the earth. Staking is the solution to part of the problem, and there are various methods, depending on the type of tree and its location. There is now sound evidence to suggest that trees are better *without* the traditional stake (if they can blow around a bit more, the stem becomes stronger). However, most gardeners still like to stake their trees.

Stakes are sold by garden centres, but choose pressure-treated types, where available, to ensure efficient rot protection. Alternatively, larch, spruce, or hardwoods make good stakes.

Use a proprietary horticultural preservative to treat the part of the the stake that's to be sunk in the ground, plus about 150mm (6in) above ground, making sure you thoroughly soak the wood.

Bush trees, dwarf bushes, standard and half-standard trees need what is called the 'double stake' to support them in exposed

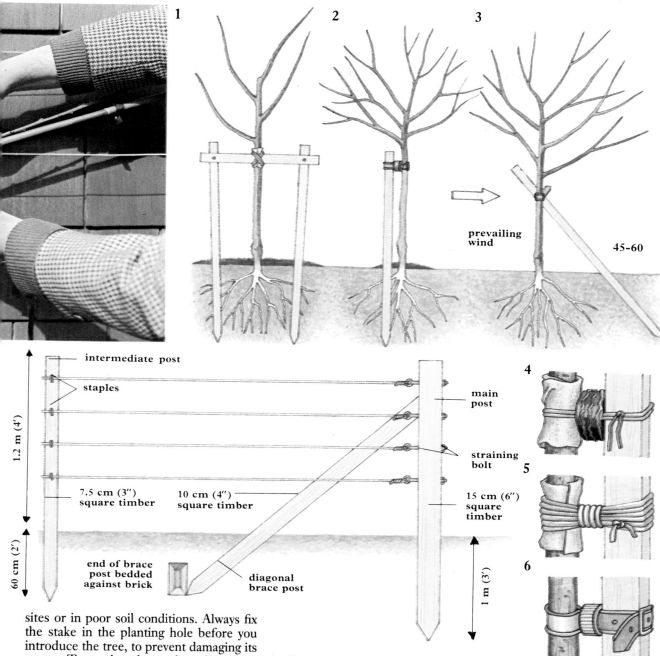

1

2

3

prevailing
wind

45-60

intermediate post

staples

1.2 m (4')

7.5 cm (3")
square timber

10 cm (4")
square timber

60 cm (2')

end of brace
post bedded
against brick

diagonal
brace post

main
post

straining
bolt

15 cm (6")
square
timber

1 m (3')

4

5

6

sites or in poor soil conditions. Always fix the stake in the planting hole before you introduce the tree, to prevent damaging its roots. To make the stake, drive two uprights into the ground about 450mm (18in), so they protrude as high as the tree's lowest branch. Screw or lash a horizontal cross-piece to each upright near the tops (you may find it easier to make up the stake before fixing it in the hole).

A single stake is suitable for supporting smaller trees. Drive the stake into the ground and secure to the stem. To support a tree that's already planted, but susceptible to damage, drive in a stake at an angle of about 45 degrees to avoid the roots, pointing towards the prevailing wind, and lash to the tree.

Exercise care in the way you tie the tree to the stake. It's important, to prevent chafing between stem and stake, to fit a buffer of some kind. Wrap a wad of hessian around the stem of the tree then wind cord around stem and stake, with the cord tied at right-angles between the two. Alternatively, tie an offcut of rubber (perhaps from an old tyre) between the tree and stake. Proprietary plastic ties are made for this purpose, if you prefer, and include a plastic buffer. These can be adjusted as the tree grows.

Wall trees also need a little extra support and this can be accomplished using horizontal wires strung across the wall between posts or threaded onto screw-in vine eyes (driven into wallplugs). If you're using wooden posts, fasten the wire using screw-in cup hooks and attach a straining bolt at one end to keep the wires taut. Use 2.50mm gauge galvanized wire.

1. *A double stake, used for standards and half-standards.*
2. *A single stake support for smaller trees.*
3. *If you need to add a stake after planting, set it at an angle to avoid the roots.*
4. *Wrap the tree with hessian and use a strip of rubber – from an old tyre – as a buffer between the stake.*
5. *Another method is to tie cord at right angles between tree and stake as a buffer.*
6. *Proprietary plastic tree ties hold the tree away from the stake and can be adjusted as it grows.*

CHAPTER 5
FURNITURE IN THE GARDEN

Furnishing your garden can be great fun, and it should be treated like a room indoors – there's furniture for dining, lounging, resting or partying. You can make it yourself or buy an entire suite.

Creating a bountiful garden has its just rewards: once the hard slog is over you can take time out to admire your handywork from the vantage of a comfortable chair. Treat the garden as an outdoor living room and furnish it accordingly. Whether you fancy just lying back with a drink or a book, dining in a shady corner, or resting briefly during a stroll, taking stock of your horticultural prowess, you'll find there's numerous pieces of furniture that's sure to fit the bill.

Narrow down the field by deciding whether your furniture is to be a permanent outdoor fixture or portable, storable units. Choose a style that complements the nature of your plot: a paved courtyard suits a fairly formal approach of elegant items; a leafy, wild setting favours the rustic touch; an airy patio suggests the plush bright approach of sociable seating. Also, choose materials shrewdly: if your furniture is to remain outdoors all year round, as often happens, it must be extremely hard-wearing and durable.

Furnishing styles
The basic bench is ideal for a quiet corner or under a tree. Proprietary types are made but it's easy enough to make one from a few stout planks on a large stone or small brick columns at each end. Park benches, with backrest and armrest, are a more formal style, which look their best against a wall, or facing a pleasant view.

The deckchair is still a popular choice for sun worshippers: it's adjustable, portable, and compact when folded. Some types even have arm rests and leg rests. Still on the collapsible front, there's the lightweight metal-framed chairs with canvas or plastic covers, or the wooden-framed, canvas-covered director's side-folding chair.

If sunbathing is your aim, a simple metal-framed, stretch-covered folding lounger will be ideal.

Folding patio suites in metal or plastic frames (and with removable upholstered cushions) are the answer to complete garden furnishing. They typically consist of, at the very least, a set of four folding chairs and a table with central parasol, but some kinds feature extras such as adjustable-position loungers, wheeled sunbeds and occasionally even a swing hammock and awning.

On a practical note, the outdoor picnicker could do no worse than invest in a trestle table with integral benches, which can seat the entire family. Some have central parasols, too.

These are just a small sample of the selection of furniture you'll find in garden centres and department stores. There are many variants in both materials used and in durability, so choose wisely.

What materials?
The best all-weather furniture is plastic, which needs little maintenance and never needs to be painted. Timber, particularly

The low rattan table and stripy deckchairs are the perfect choice in a leafy courtyard plot, whether you're dining or just languishing with a drink.

hardwood, offers better quality but requires regular attention to fend off rot. Softwoods (with the exception of cedar) must be treated with preservatives to withstand the elements.

Rust is the main enemy of metal furniture, although galvanizing, painting and plastic coatings will keep this menace at bay, so long as the surface isn't scratched or chipped. Aluminium is the saving grace as far as metal furniture is concerned; it doesn't rust, is lighter than steel and can be cast – like iron – to make ornately moulded tables and chairs reminiscent of a Victorian garden.

Regular maintenance

With a little care and attention your garden furniture will last for years. Unless it's the outdoor type, it's best to store the furniture in a well-ventilated shed or garage during the summer but to bring it indoors in the winter.

Lubricate all pivots, hinges, and screw heads with thin oil to discourage rust and ensure good working order. Smear metal-framed chairs with oil each winter and wipe off before use the next season. Treat exposed softwoods with colourless preservative each year, just before the summer season. Hardwood may need staining or varnishing.

Fitting new covers

Fabric-covered chairs are prone to splits and tears, particularly at pressure points, but in most cases it's possible to patch them up.

Pull together the torn fabric, fold over the frayed edges and stitch together using 60-gauge thread. Fit a patch of matching material over the rent and stitch it in place. Tears at seams can be stitched back together also: overstitch for strength, and carry the stitching beyond the extent of the rent.

When a fabric cover is beyond repair, you can fit a replacement. Deckchairs can be refitted with rotproof synthetic coverings (available from hardware stores in standard 445mm (17½in) widths, often in pre-cut lengths). Use the old cover as a template for the new one. Remove it by prising off its tacks with an old screwdriver.

Lay the deckchair on the floor and fold over one end of the new fabric by 25mm (1in). Fold it around the top rail and tack it to the underside of the rail. With the deckchair erected and inverted, pull the fabric around the bottom rail; this is narrower than the top rail, so fold in each side of the fabric to form a taper. Fold over the end 25mm (1in) and tack the fold to the inside edge of the rail.

Collapsible metal chairs can be recovered

similarly. Remove the damaged covering by cutting through the stitching with a sharp knife. Use the old cover to buy a new matching replacement then, with the chair open, drape the new fabric over the top bar. Fold under 12mm (½in) and backstich the fold to the cover fabric using 60-gauge thread. Make a double stitch at each end for strength. Pull the fabric behind the metal tensioning bar at the back of the seat and over the front bar. Fold the strip around with a 12mm (½in) overlap and pin it to the fabric. Test the folding action of the chair to make sure the fabric is properly tensioned then backstitch along the front fold and remove the pins.

A common problem with folding sun loungers is that the support cords, which stretch the fabric over the frame, often snap. Repair kits are available: they comprise a set of strong rubber bands and metal hooks. Remove the broken cord, which is laced between eyes in side flaps. Fit a hook at each end of a band and stretch these between the side flaps, fitting the hooks in the eyes. Work right from the centre eye outwards.

A raised sundeck with built-in bench seating and boxy armchairs made entirely from planks is one solution for an awkward plot, or if you can't spare much time to garden. The barbecue area, with comfy seating, allows the tree access, lending a natural look to the scheme.

CHAPTER 6

TOOLS, MACHINERY & MAINTENANCE

No gardener can cope without a reliable set of tools. Equip yourself with the best you can afford and then tend them scrupulously so they won't let you down. And for that special job that demands a special touch, a visit to your local hire shop will suffice.

You can't tame your jungle of weeds without an adequate kit of good quality weaponry. Unless you make a point of regularly maintaining your tools, they'll soon fall foul of your neglect. But even the best-tended implements will succumb to years of hard labour, and minor repairs will be necessary to revive them.

Mechanical or electric-powered tools are an integral part of the modern gardener's equipment and they demand special care to ensure reliable working and assure safety to the user. If you prefer, most of the heavy, specialist equipment, that you will probably not use very often, is available through hire shops.

Maintaining garden tools

A few months of hard labour in the garden can leave your tools looking a little jaded, but don't just dump them in the shed for the winter without sparing them some attention.

Rust is the worst offender: it attacks anything made of iron and steel and can have a devastating effect if left unchecked. It is quite easy to inhibit the rust from forming in the first place by practising just a few simple, but extremely worthwhile preventative measures.

Regular tool care

Before you put your tools away, make sure they're clean and dry: caked-on mud, full of moisture, will soon promote an unhealthy rust to form on spade blades and fork tines. Wipe this off as soon as you've finished digging.

If you spot any signs of rust, rub them down with wire wool and daub the affected metal with oil or grease. Before you put your tools away into winter storage, spray all metal parts with a proprietary moisture-dispersing lubricant, or coat them in oil or grease. Dismantle any mechanical gadgets and give their components a thorough cleaning. Reassemble them, lubricating the working parts.

The garden shed isn't the best place to store rust-prone tools and equipment. Unless the walls are adequately lined with building paper (which discourages condensation) and the doors and windows are properly insulated against draughts, tools will quickly rust in the damp conditions. Where feasible, it's best to bring your portable tools indoors during winter. Keep them in a warm cupboard (under the stairs for instance).

This may be out of the question, of course: if you've no alternative store-room than the shed, do your best to improve the environment inside. Place small hand tools (screwdrivers, trowels, hammers) in a drawer or box (left slightly open for good air flow). Wrap the metal parts (which should be oiled or greased) in special waxed rust-inhibiting paper (available from builders' merchants) secured with elastic bands. Line the drawer or box with the paper, too. Long-handled tools can be hung up on the walls, with the metal parts wrapped in rust-inhibiting paper.

Small precision tools, tiny spanners, keys for tool adjustment, junior hacksaw blades, and drill bits can be kept in a sealed jam-jar that contains a little silica gel, a substance that drives off moisture. You can buy this from builders' merchants and chemists and is commonly used between the panes of secondary double glazing to dispel moisture.

Rot is the other enemy of garden tools: unvarnished wood such as the handles of some tools is prone to attack. Apply a light coating of linseed oil with a rag, to feed the wood and keep it supple. Leave the oil to soak in and repeat the treatment every few months.

Power tools can be dangerous if allowed to deteriorate, so check the condition of their flexes thoroughly for fraying and

Opposite *Keep your lawn a cut above the rest by maintaining your lawnmower regularly. Clean the blades, oil the moving parts and adjust the height of cut to suit the length of the grass you are mowing.*

splits. If there's the slightest sign of damage, renew the flex immediately. Examine the plug also: dismantle it and remake the connections so you're sure everything's sound. Re-examine at the beginning of the work season.

Curing the rust menace

When you've failed to pamper your tools and they've become the victims of an attack by rust, there's still time to make amends. Scrape off any loose, flaky rust with a wire brush then daub on a generous amount of a proprietary rust-killing chemical. These substances (either a liquid or a jelly) are usually based on phosphoric acid, which combines with the rust and makes it largerly inert. Most types prime the metal ready for repainting.

Repairing broken handles

Wooden handles on tools are fairly tough and durable but not if you misuse them. Trying to lever out too much earth when you're deep-digging in the garden is a sure way to fracture the shaft of a spade or fork, while the thinner handles of rakes and hoes will snap if left lying around and then inadvertently stepped on.

Use one of the standard-diameter handles that are available for repairing broken shafts. Long-handled tools have handles that fit in a socket formed in the top of the tool's blade; smaller tools such as

hand forks and trowels have handles that are stuck on the end of a metal tang.

New handles are usually supplied longer and thicker at the socket end than you actually need; you'll have to cut them to size and shape them to a tight fit.

The point where the shaft enters the metal socket is where the most strain is applied, and the area most likely to snap. If this happens, you have the problem of extracting the stub of the shaft from the socket. The shaft will probably be retained by a screw or rivet, and this must be removed first. Lay the tool on a flat surface, or clamp in the jaws of a vice or workbench. Withdraw the screw, applying pressure if necessary, to loosen it: if it's rusted in, soak with penetrating oil then try again. Really stubborn screws (and rivets) must be drilled out using a high speed drill bit.

If you can't get a grip on the shaft stub, drive a large 75mm (3in) No. 12 screw into the end of the stub, clamp the screw in a vice with the tool's blade hanging down, then strike the top of the blade with a mallet to pull it free.

Saw the new shaft to length then use the old stub as a template for marking the taper on the end. Place the stub end onto the new handle and draw around it. Clamp the shaft in a vice and plane down the end to the correct taper using a planer file or spoke-shave. It's a good idea to leave the taper slightly oversize for a really tight fit.

Even the most basic tools need special care and attention: here a garden roller is give a dose of oil to prevent its drum from rusting.

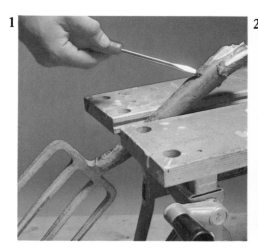

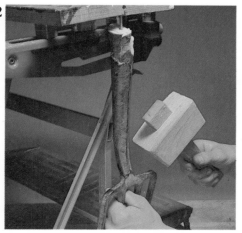

1. *Remove the broken shaft of a fork or spade by releasing its retaining screw — you may have to drill out a rivet instead.*
2. *Drive a screw into the end of the shaft stub, clamp in a vice or workbench and release the head by tapping with a mallet.*
3. *Use the old stub of the shaft to mark the length and amount of taper you'll need to cut from the replacement shaft.*
4. *Shave the end of the new shaft to the diameter you want using a small planer file, spokeshave or wood rasp, so that it fits in the head socket snugly.*
5. *Force the shaft into the socket then secure with a new galvanized screw driven in through the hole in the socket.*
6. *Before you store away metal tools, coat them liberally with mosture-dispersing lubricant to prevent rust and keep moving parts well oiled.*

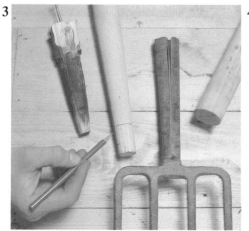

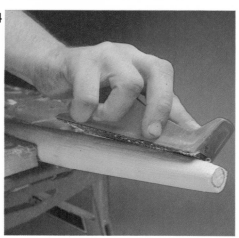

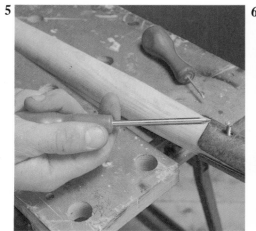

Slot the shaft into the tool's socket and align the grip with the blade. Rest the blade on a block of wood then tap the grip end to force the shape into the socket. To secure the shaft, first drill a 2mm (1/16in) pilot hole through the socket hole and drive in a screw.

Sharpening blunt shears

Garden shears will become blunt with frequent use, and you can sharpen them yourself if the cutting edge isn't too badly nicked (if the blades are badly damaged, leave the job to a specialist tool sharpener).

Sharpen each blade separately for con-venient working. Remove the pivot bolt and clamp one blade in a vice. Examine the cutting edge: some blades are steeply angled, others are shallow. When you're resharpening, follow the original profile. Use a fine flat metalworking file (held at an angle of about 15 degrees for a steep angle) and file away from the edge. Work along the full length of the blade to restore its cutting edge. Repeat for the other blade, reassemble the tool and test its cutting action.

Shears cut with a scissor action and the cross-over set of the blades is important. Hold the tool upright and look at the side:

1. *If garden shears don't cut properly, check the tips – they should meet. Cure the problems by filling down the back stops. Remove only a little metal, then test the cut; repeat if necessary.*
2. *To sharpen the shears, separate the blades, clamp in a vice and file, using a fine metalworking file, to restore the edge to its original cutting angle.*

the blades should bow inwards towards the points and some only touch at the very ends. If the blades don't bow, try tightening the pivot bolt with a screwdriver to correct the fault. Hold the tool by one handle: if the blades open of their own accord, they should be correctly set. Failing this, dismantle the tool and clamp each blade upright in a vice, one at a time, and bend the tip gently. Reassemble the shears and test the cut. The blades should cross over for their entire length.

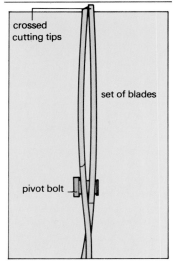

crossed
cutting tips

set of blades

pivot bolt

Right *The blades of a pair of hand shears, if they're to cut properly, should cross over for their entire length. Look along the edge of the closed shears: the blades should bow and touch at the tips.*

A gap near the tips of the blades signifies that the 'stops' behind the pivot bolt are meeting too soon. Dismantle the tool and then carefully file down each stop just fractionally to correct the fault.

Lawnmowers

The lawnmower is probably one of the most frequently-used items of garden equipment during the grass-growing season: the rest of the time it stands idle, often in a damp shed, frequently caked in dried grass cuttings.

Apart from regular cleaning, basic maintenance (adjusting and sharpening the blades, lubricating the moving parts) is called for to keep your lawnmower running efficiently. Whatever type of machine you have, some procedures are common to all.

Types of lawnmower

You'll be spoilt for choice when buying a new mower – there's one to cope with every size and shape of lawn, from the tiny, flat pocket handkerchief to the undulating meadow. Initially you'll have to decide between hand-powered, electrical or petrol-engined types, then consider one of three basic cutting systems:
● **Cylinder mowers** have cutting blades fixed to a cylinder, which revolves at right-angles to the grass surface. A roller behind produces the familiar striped effect, by 'flattening' the grass in alternate directions in each row. They're either hand-operated or motor-driven, and usually have a grass-collecting box.
● **Rotary mowers** have a single bar blade, or rectangular or circular disc cutters fixed to a disc that revolves parallel to the grass. All rotary mowers are motor-driven and can tackle coarse lawns.

● **Hover mowers** are really variants of the rotary action, but float above the grass on a cushion of air. Highly maneouvrable, they're also light in weight and some models feature a grass box. Hover types can be driven electrically or by a petrol engine.

Manual models are really only viable for a small, flat lawn; lightweight electrics are good here, too, but choose a larger electric model for a medium-sized plot; petrol types deal with large areas where a trailing lead would be impractical; hover mowers can be used successfully on any size of lawn but excel on steep slopes and rough terrain.

Maintenance checklist

A simple checklist of likely trouble spots will enable you to prolong the working life of the mower. Before you start, however, make sure a powered mower is unplugged before you touch the moving parts.

● Before you start to mow, check that the height-of-cut adjusters are equal.

● Clean the blades after each mowing to remove caked-on cuttings from the deflector plate and long strands wound round the rotating parts, typically the main roller and the cylinder blade bearings.

● Lightly oil the height adjusters and clean and generously oil the cylinder blade bearings.

● On a cylinder mower, check that the cutting blades are sound. Hold a metal straightedge or ruler against the fixed bottom blade to highlight distortions; gently tap the blade with a hammer to re-align it. If it's very worn, buy and fit a new one.

● Before you put the mower away for the season, examine the drive chain compartment: remove its cover by loosening the self-tapping screws, or bolts and check the state of the nylon chain tensioner. Lubricate it and the gear teeth and chain then replace the cover.

Adjusting cylinder blades

The cylinder mower is one of the most popular models. It has two sets of blades: a fixed bottom blade, and a rotating blade that cuts against the fixed one. The height of the grass cut is determined by the height of the fixed blade from the ground. To adjust this to suit, it's usual to alter the

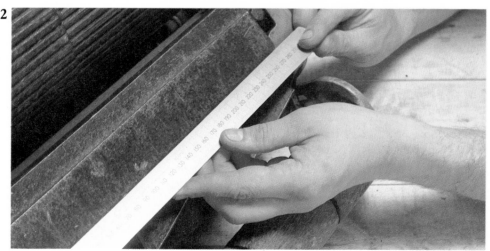

1. Adjust the height of cut on a cylinder mower by altering the level of the roller. Slacken the side nuts and alter either end by the same amount, using a spanner.
2. Use a metal ruler to check that the cylinder and fixed blades of the mower are not bent.

1. *To adjust the cylinder blade in relation to the fixed blade, support the rollers off the ground with a wooden wedge, so you can turn the blades freely.*
2. *Gradually tighten both adjusting screws in turn until the blades will cut cleanly through a sheet of cartridge paper placed between the bottom blade and the cylinder blades.*
3. *To sharpen the cylinder blades using the backlapping technique, adjust the cylinder and bottom blade until they touch or until they can trap a sheet of thin paper placed between them.*
4. *Smear coarse grinding paste onto each blade in turn then turn the cylinder backwards to sharpen the blades. Adjust both sides as you go.*

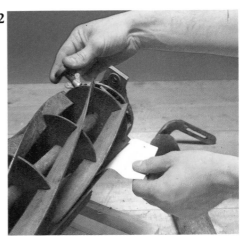

height of the front roller, which raises or lowers the mower body accordingly. This will either be accomplished on modern machines by flipping two levers into channels at each side or, on older types, by loosening a nut at each side and sliding the roller's brackets up or down.

To cut the grass properly the fixed blade and the rotary blade must be the correct distance apart: too close and they'll bind; too far apart and the grass will remain standing. Most mowers have a screw adjuster on each side of the cylinder case and by releasing these, it's possible to alter the positions of the blades. Lay the mower on its back to gain access to the fixed blade, then adjust the screws in turn to move the rotary blade. Test the cut by feeding a sheet of thickish paper between fixed and moveable blades; it should cut cleanly. Tighten the lock nuts and test the mower.

Sharpening cylinder blades

Mower blades meet all sorts of obstructions on their travels – not least of which are stones, which can ruin a cutting edge instantly. The rotary blades of a cylinder mower can be sharpened by grinding them against the fixed blade, so long as the latter is not worn unevenly. If it is, replace it first.

To be able to turn the blades you'll have

to remove the gear or chain plate at the side of the mower and disconnect the drive from the roller to the cylinder (this may be a small gear wheel or a chain). If it's a chain, find the connector link and prise off its spring clip or split pin and slide the gear off the shaft. It should now be possible to turn the cylinder with a ratchet or box spanner held on the cylinder gear locking nuts.

With some models of mower the job's much simpler: just turning the roller backwards turns the cylinder blade.

With either method, raise up the mower so the cylinder can be turned freely, and adjust the bottom blade and cylinder so they just meet. Smear a little coarse grinding paste (you can buy this from motoring accessory shops) onto the cutting edge of each blade. To sharpen, turn the cylinder backwards. As you grind you should examine the blades to make sure they're evenly in contact. Once you can see a continuous ground line on each blade, wipe off the paste and reassemble the mower.

Sharpening rotary blades

The other popular mower is the rotary-action type, in which a single, double-edged blade or series of disc-shaped or rectangular blades spin parallel to the ground. The same problem common to other mowers is the damage stones and other obstructions can do to the cutting edge. But, similarly, sharpening a blunt blade is quite straightforward.

Rotary bar blades are fixed centrally to a rotating disc by a single bolt. Grasp one end of the blade with a wad of cloths and use a hexagonal spanner to undo the bolt. Most mowers come with a suitable spanner. Remove the bolt and its spacer discs (which are used to alter the cutting height) noting which way up it goes. Take the opportunity to clean and grease the mounting and bolt.

Clamp the blade horizontally in a vice and grind the first cutting edge sharp with a fine flat metalworking file. Repeat for the cutting edge on the diagonally opposite end of the bar. The blade must be balanced to work properly: check this by fixing a large nail into a post or wall and slot the blade onto it. The end that drops is heavier and you'll have to file the back of this end until the bar balances.

Refit the bar blade with spacers (the more you add the shorter the grass will be cut), and the central bolt.

Some rotary bar blades have detachable triangular cutting edges bolted onto the ends. Blade ends aren't easy to sharpen, so it's best to replace them with new ones. Release their nuts and bolts and fit the replacements, making sure their cutting edges are facing the direction of rotation.

Some rotary mowers have bar blades with two diagonally opposite corners turned up to create a draught in rotation, which disperses the grass cuttings. Both ends must be balanced or vibration could damage the mower's engine. Remove the blade and file the heavier end, as previously described.

When a circular disc blade becomes blunt, loosen its fixing and swivel it to present a new cutting edge.

1 To sharpen a rotary mower blade, unplug the mower, upend, then undo the bolt in the centre of the rotating disc – hold one end of the blade with a rag to stop the blade from turning.

2 Remove the bolt and spacer washers that secure the blade. Take note of which way up the blade is fixed. Clean the mounting and thoroughly grease the securing bolt.

3 Clamp the blade in a vice and use a fine engineering file to sharpen the blade to the original cutting angle – if it's badly gouged or blunted, it's easiest to buy a replacement.

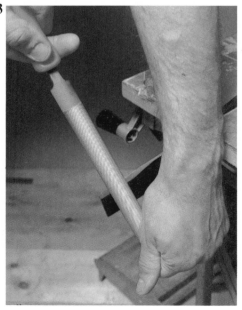

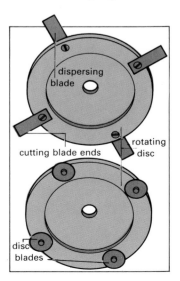

Far left Two other types of rotary mower blades: rectangular cutting blade ends fixed to the rotating disc, and disc blades. Some can be turned to reveal new cutting edges, others must be replaced when blunt.

Obtain specialist tools from a tool hire shop, where trained staff will be able to guide you to just the item you want to make the job that much easier.

Hiring and using machinery

Substantial alterations to your garden – terracing, levelling, drain-laying (see pages 6–11) – or other large-scale tasks that involve a lot of hard, physical labour, will doubtless tax the abilities of your meagre gardening tools, to say nothing of your strength and stamina.

Often there's a tool or piece of equipment that would enable you to get on with the job at twice the pace. In some cases it might be worthwhile investing in such an item, but the chances are it's something so specialized (or expensive) that you're unlikely to ever to have need for it again, The solution is to hire what you need.

Buy or hire?

General tools such as electric drills and hedgetrimmers, and equipment such as a wheelbarrow and workbench, should be bought rather than hired. You'll be able to use these over and over again and they'll be ready to hand. Although their initial outlay may be considerable, they'll pay for themselves in the long run. Consider buying second-hand tools (scour local newspapers and shop-window advertisements for bargains), with the view to selling them on when you've exhausted their use, without too much financial loss.

Save the hiring for one-off jobs you're never going to repeat, or where you need a particularly specialist or expensive item. If you're taking over a virgin plot of land with a new house, or a previously neglected site, for instance, you'll probably need heavy-weight mechanized assistance: obviously, purchasing these items would be prohibitive.

Where to hire

There are many specialist tool hire shops, some of which belong to nationwide chains; others are local business operated by the proprietor. Shops that are part of a large chain usually offer a greater selection of equipment and can often order certain items from other branches if they don't have what you want themselves. Most shops will supply comprehensive lists or catalogues of their stock, along with hire charges.

Garden tools and equipment are often hired out by larger garden centres but substantial jobs requiring very large machines are probably best obtained from a plant hire company or general building contractor.

It's usually possible to hire over the telephone, and advance ordering is often necessary for the popular items.

Hire charges

Tools and equipment are usually hired out at an hourly, daily, weekly or monthly rate (although some hire for periods of four or eight hours rather than a whole day) and the scale of charges is frequently complex. Make sure you find out exactly what you'll have to pay.

Clarify the exact period you'll be charged for and find out if you can save money if you return the tools before the hire period expires.

Weekly hire charges usually reflect about ten per cent of the new purchase price of the tool, so use this equation as a basis for comparing charges between hirers: they can vary considerably. You'll discover that it's cheaper to hire for one week rather than for three days or more, and that some equipment can't be hired for less than a week.

A deposit will be demanded on each item you hire, which is to ensure that it will be returned undamaged; it pays you to take care when using the tools, or you could lose the deposit. The deposit might equal about three weeks' hire, and is usually acceptable in the form of a cheque (or credit card), which is returned to you later, or deducted from the rental cost.

Most hire shops will deliver the tools and equipment, for which there'll be an extra charge, so it makes sense to collect and return them yourself (but don't be tempted to overload your car or transport anything in a dangerous condition).

The hire charges come into effect as soon as you leave the premises with the goods (or when they're delivered), so make fullest use of the time: don't allow the gear to stand idle.

The hire contract

When you hire you'll have to provide positive proof of identity (a driving licence,

for instance) and you'll be required to sign an agreement, which binds you by law to the terms laid down, usually in small print on the back. Read this carefully.

Basically you'll be acknowledging that you've inspected the goods and have found them in good order, that you've been instructed in its use, and that you undertake to return it in a 'clean and serviceable condition'. You're responsible for the safe keeping of the hired goods (check that it's covered by your house contents policy if it's stolen): the hirer isn't responsible for damage or personal injury caused by the equipment, unless it's proved that the hire company is negligent.

Therefore, it's sensible to examine the items you're hiring and make sure you're supplied with detailed instructions for use.

What can be hired?

The types of tools and equipment available for hire fall into three basic catagories: they're either manually-operated, petrol-driven, or electrically-powered (although some larger machines are diesel-powered).

If you're reclaiming an overgrown, debris-strewn site, there are many tools available for hire to help you clear up: as far as hand tools go, you can choose from a selection of

Bottom left *A stake driver being used to drive a timber stake into the ground. This tool is especially useful if you have a lot of supports to fix for fruit trees, or when building a fruit cage.*

Below *A selection of useful hand tools available for hire for the garden handyman:*
1. *An extendable pruning saw is an invaluable aid if you have to prune tall trees from ground level.*
2. *The scythe is still one of the most efficient tools for cutting long grass.*
3. *A hedge knife, or slasher, is good for cutting back unruly hedges or bushes.*
4. *A sickle will tackle long grass and weeds in the most inaccessible parts.*

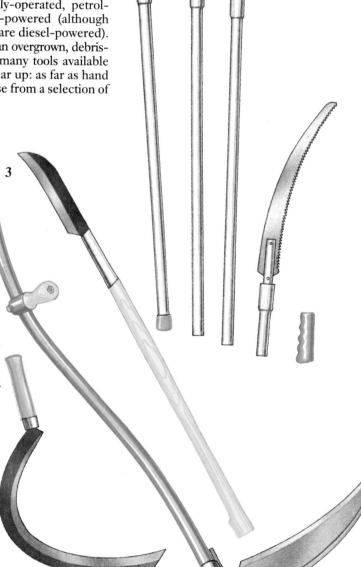

A power chain saw makes tree-felling simple, so long as you're very careful to use it following the maker's safety instructions. Petrol driven, it's supremely portable.

traditional sickles and scythes to cope with cutting long grasses, nettles and other weeds, and a billhook or pruning saw for trimming and pruning trees and bushes. Exercise great care when using sharp tools such as these. Motor scythes are also available.

A long-handled axe is a simple but effective way to fell even fairly stout trees (be sure to choose an axe with a suitable weight; light is best if you're a newcomer to this work). For lighter tree-felling opt for a double-handed saw, which requires two people to operate, each pulling – never pushing – the blade.

A chain-saw, petrol or electric-powered, will make short shrift of tree trunks and branches, but you must be cautious when using it: it's a lethal tool if misused. Always use with the guard in position. Never cut towards your body or limbs. Choose a blade size to suit the stock of timber you're likely to be cutting: widths vary from 450mm (18in) to 750mm (30in). A petrol version is best where you're remote from a power supply.

A winch or block-and-tackle is a saviour when you're removing small trees and bushes, or rocks that are too unwieldy to dig out, and powered versions are available for hire.

Where you have a lot of builder's rubble to break up, use a simple pick-axe, or a powered jack hammer for extensive work. Persistent weeds can be destroyed using a flame gun, but only where there's plenty of space (and even then an appropriate weed-killer will probably do the job more efficiently).

Once you've cleared your site you can begin to establish some order. Hire a skip from a specialist skip hire company to dispose of all the debris. Skips (delivered on the back of a special lorry) can be left on your drive or, with permission from the local authority, on the highway outside your house, space permitting, and so long as it's lit at night. The skip company will probably arrange this for you.

If you need to erect boundary fences, hire a post-hole borer to excavate the holes for the posts. The tool is easy to use. It has a corkscrew-like blade, that is simply driven into the ground by turning the handle at the top. When the correct depth is reached, you lift the borer out, complete with earth.

Stake drivers are used similarly, for forcing posts and stakes into the ground for supporting fencing or other structures, in a very short time.

Drainage improvements in the garden (see pages 8–11) are extremely laborious if you have a network of trenches to dig for the pipes. The same applies for burying electric cables for an outdoor power supply, so in either case you'll find a trench digger the speedy, easy way to get the job done. The machine consists of a continuous belt to which are attached a number of scoops, which shovel out the earth to the depth and width you want.

Soil cultivation is another back-breaking job if you try to tackle it with only hand tools. Powered cultivators can be hired, and will cope with major digging in a large vegetable plot; the rotary cultivator, a version with tines or hoe-blades to do the digging, is eminently suited to general garden excavating. But be warned that if the ground is full of perennial weeds, a rotary cultivator could propagate some of them by chopping up the roots and spreading them around.

If you find digging with a spade a very tedious chore, you can even hire a special spade that lifts the laden blade by a powerful spring and flips over the earth. An interchangeable fork head is also supplied with the tool.

When you start to furnish your new garden with paths, steps, patio and garden buildings, you'll probably find yourself mixing a lot of concrete to make various bases (see pages 34–35). Motorized mixers save much time and effort in blending the ingredients, and there's one ingenious portable mixer that you fill up, tip onto integral wheels and take for a walk around the garden to mix the concrete as the drum revolves.

The general construction of fences, walls, pergolas and other structures calls for a comprehensive supply of general woodworking and building tools, which you'd be well advised to collect yourself – but rest assured, if there's something you need which you'd rather not buy, it will almost certainly be available from a hire shop.

Even when your garden is established, you'll probably still be visiting the hire shop for its range of soil-care equipment which includes such items as sterilizers, fertilizer mixers and distributors. Seed distributors and powerful insecticide sprayers are also available to ease and certainly speed up your gardening chores.

Above *A concrete mixer you can take for a walk: this clever device makes mixing by hand easy.*

Left *A lightweight, four-stroke petrol engined 'boom' type cultivator is highly manoeuvrable and ideal for the smaller plots.*

Left *A larger 'drag shoe' cultivator will cope with a large plot with ease.*

INDEX